GW01454510

# From Desp

# to Hope

**A Christian perspective
on the tragedy of suicide**

*Meara*

Council on Social Responsibilty
Methodist Church in Ireland

*VERITAS*

*Published 2002 by*
Veritas Publications
7/8 Lower Abbey Street
Dublin 1
Email publications@veritas.ie
Website www.veritas.ie

ISBN 1 85390 672 7

A catalogue record for this book is available from the British Library.

Contact for the working group who drew up this report:
Robert Cochran
Secretary
Methodist Council on Social Responsibility
63 Lynwood
Dublin 16
rcochran@indigo.ie

Cover design by Louise Baker
Printed in the Republic of Ireland by Leinster Leader Ltd, Dublin

*Veritas books are printed on paper made from the wood pulp of managed forests. For every tree felled, at least one tree is planted, thereby renewing natural resources*

# CONTENTS

**Part II
Responding as Individuals**

**Part III**
**Responding as Churches**

*To all those who have been bereaved through suicide*

*To the memory of those, especially within the life of the churches, who have ended their lives by suicide*

# PREFACE

This book has been produced by the Council on Social Responsibility of the Methodist Church in Ireland, as a study and information resource for those working with and concerned for the tragedy of those for whom life has no longer any meaning. The Council is the body within the Methodist Church that seeks to reflect from a Christian perspective on issues of concern in the social, economic and political sphere. From that, it seeks to guide and inform the Church membership in relation to such matters, and also to articulate the Church's stance to the wider community. This report thus unambiguously approaches the subject of suicide from a perspective of Christian concern.

*From Despair to Hope* has had a long gestation. We, like many other groups in society, have been increasingly concerned by the growing incidence of suicide. Guided by the working group appointed to examine this issue, we started on a journey of exploration, information, understanding and hopefully insight, which has finally culminated in this publication.

This book is intended as material for discussion by clergy and lay pastoral workers; lay leaders; concerned lay women and men; concerned youth groups; survivors; family friends and colleagues, and of course, despite its origins, not only by those within the Methodist tradition. It is not intended as a medical or sociological textbook, nor does it attempt to be comprehensive. Rather it aims to present information relevant to those in pastoral and counselling situations. A selected list of sources of further information and support are outlined in the Appendix for those seeking further advice and assistance.

We want particularly to acknowledge the expertise and hard work of the Council Working Group who undertook the bulk of the work from which this report arises and who formed the editorial team. We were fortunate to have people with such a relevant range of experience and expertise. These are: Dr Edith Loane, psychiatrist (especially chapters three and nine); Rev Katherine Meyer, student chaplain (especially chapters two and four); Joan Rippingale, counsellor (especially chapter two); Tony Walsh, clinical psychologist and bereavement counsellor (especially chapters one, two, six and part of nine).

In addition, parts of the report were written by others with relevant experience, for which we are grateful and thankful. These are: May Anderson (chapter eight), Berta Armitage (part of chapter two), Rev. Sydney Callaghan and Salters Sterling (chapter five), Rev David Neilands (part of chapter seven), Pam Stotter (chapter nine), Malcolm Brown and Heather Ferguson-Brown (part of chapter seven). We are also particularly pleased that these inputs have come from across the spectrum of Christian traditions.

*Robert Cochran*
*Secretary*
*Council on Social Responsibility*
*Methodist Church in Ireland*

# PART 1

# UNDERSTANDING SUICIDE

*This first section outlines the current situation with regard to suicide and puts it into context. It then seeks to illustrate the wide range of circumstances in which suicide may occur though the medium of a series of stories based on real experiences, with some reflection on each.*

1. Suicide in Context

2. Personal Stories

3. Social and High-Risk Factors

# SUICIDE IN CONTEXT

## 1.1    Setting the Scene

The preventative approaches [to suicide] ... must involve all sections of society in a multiplicity of inter-related activities and responses. It is only in this manner that the possibility of solutions to the problem of suicide will evolve.

*(Report of the Irish National Task Force on Suicide)*

Accompanying the rapid social changes that have been central to Irish society in recent years, there has been a dramatic shift in both the rates and the patterns of suicide. Some decades ago Ireland had one of the lowest suicide rates in Europe. This has changed significantly over the last twenty years. There were over 300 suicides in 1991, 478 in 1997 and 413 in 2000 in the Republic. The figures peaked in 1998 at 504. This implies that some 2,500 people were directly affected and some 60,000 people's lives were touched by suicide in that year.

Northern Ireland Samaritans also report dramatic increases. Comparison with figures for other European countries indicate similar trends. While the main shift has been a significant increase in numbers, most noticeably among young people and more particularly among young men, a number of other significant trends also emerge from an analysis of such figures. These deserve attention.

- The suicide rate for men in Ireland is double that for women.
- The most significant occupational group among male suicides in the 1990s were farmers.
- The rate for young men aged between fifteen and twenty-four is three times higher than it was twenty years ago in the Republic, while in the UK it has increased by 75 per cent since 1982.
- The most significant group among women suicides in the 1990s were full-time homemakers.
- It is hypothesised that the rate for gay or lesbian young people may be two or three times higher than for their heterosexual peers.
- Research has shown a positive correlation between alcohol and substance abuse; recent studies suggest that this is particularly significant in areas of Belfast.
- In general, suicides rates for those over sixty-five years of age are very significantly higher than for the population as a whole.

These figures are accompanied by a dramatic increase in para-suicides – those attempts to end life that either consciously or unconsciously do not succeed in completing the act. The multiplication in destructive behaviour patterns such as drug dependency and alcohol abuse are also significant. All this is taking place within the context of Irish society both North and South of the border, where there has been profound change in social edifices, community coherence, family structures, societal values and religious practice.

Emile Durkheim, the French sociologist whose seminal writing on the subject earned him the not entirely enviable title of 'father of suicidology', suggests that changes in the fabric of society and an increase in the suicide rate should not be seen as unexpected. When societal norms and structures change or disappear then the rate of suicide tends to rise. What distinguished his study of the area, and indeed his methodological stance, was his concern not so much with the individual who takes their own life, but with the idea that such actions always take place within a range of influential societal contexts. Different societies have varying rates of suicide at varying times because of the nature of what is going on within them.

James Hillman, a Jungian analyst, in his book Suicide and the Soul concurs with Durkheim in inviting those who take the subject of suicide seriously to attend to the 'outsider' view of societal analysis and sociological enquiry. He also, however, emphasises the vital importance of the 'insider' view of the suicidal individual's reality. Every act of suicide, or para-suicide, is a deeply meaningful personal response to a set of circumstances that that individual has encountered. In analysing or seeking to understand suicide and the changing trends associated with it, we must look not just at the 'micro' of individuals or of the 'macro' of sociological process, but at the intricate web of individual and social realities that inform the complex process that create both a sense of secure identity and a rich and fulfilling experience of life.

In this analysis it is important to consider levels of social structure and support, societal norms and taboos, gender issues, educational and vocational opportunity, the presence or lack of belief in meaning systems, which give a sense value to life, and the whole area of social, cultural and economic change. For instance, to understand the huge increase in suicide among young men in West Belfast it is necessary to explore patterns of social deprivation, limited educational and vocational opportunities, unemployment, substance abuse and change in family structures. It is also essential to consider the effects of the peace process, which, while creating a wider sense of national security, may have undermined the clear social structure and sense of ideological cause established by the paramilitaries. The latter seemed to have supplied many young men with a sense of identity, meaning and social validation often lacking in a socially deprived context.

The Methodist Church, in common with the other denominations in Ireland, has a significant number of members or adherents whose lives have been touched by suicide. There are also those among us for whom suicide has been, or seems to be, the only viable choice in the face of the particular circumstances that confront them. Our churches also exist in wider communities where suicide is increasingly experienced as a disturbing reality. Central to an understanding of the New Testament concept of 'church', either local or national, is the idea of community that offers a radical and meaningful alternative value system and way of being in the world. If we are true to our calling to be a healing influence within society, to be part of the solution rather than part of the problem, then we must begin to respond to the Gospel invitation to create a radical analysis of, and a range of meaningful responses to, the problems of our era. However, in order to respond we must first understand.

## 1.2    Historical Perspectives and Suicide

Western civilisations have inherited a vein of negative reactions to suicide that still inform much of our thinking today. Ireland is no exception to this. Frequently such attitudes and reactions reside partially outside our awareness and affect our reactions at an unconscious level. It is only as we begin to trace the historical thought legacies that inform our thinking, that we can begin to make sense of the attitudes and prejudices that inform our reactions both to suicide and to those who are most closely affected by it. It is difficult to break with longstanding traditions or ways of interpreting events, particularly if we do not recognise what these are or how and why they influence our thinking and behaviour.

Many early tribal societies abhorred the act of suicide – seeing it as the ultimate threat to the tribe, its way of life and indeed its very survival. Taking your own life was the ultimate statement of individuality which was seen as undermining the idea of collectivity and group responsibility. If everyone made such individualistic statements, then tribes that depended on members working together and sacrificing their sense of individual right and autonomy could not survive and the very fabric of society would be threatened. Thus suicide was highly taboo and the bodies of those who had ended their own life were treated with execration, often being mutilated, desecrated and ultimately unceremoniously dumped outside tribal boundaries. The time-honoured rituals around death were forbidden. Gradually an element of the magical also became associated with the corpse, which itself came to be treated with dread and fear. This found expression in ritual burnings or in the removal of head, feet or hands in the hope of minimising the possibility of the person walking again or of their exerting an influence on the living. In some cultures the bodies of suicides were buried under large mounds or hills as it was felt that this might limit their ability to walk abroad as malevolent spirits.

The Roman civilisation had a somewhat different view of suicide. In certain circumstances such an end to life was seen as both honourable and desirable. In more recent times Japanese society saw suicide as a way of redeeming the life of the individual from disgrace following a scandal. Recent spates of suicide bombings also indicate that in some cultures and in certain circumstances suicide is seen as both acceptable and honourable.

While there are five suicides mentioned in the Bible, four in the Old Testament (Samson, Saul, Abimilech and Ahithophel) and one in the New Testament (Judas Iscariot) none of these acts merit particular condemnation. Nonetheless, in the first half of the first millennium the Christian Church began to evolve a deeply negative attitude – those who committed suicide were seen as condemned to eternal torment in hell and were frequently refused Christian burial. There was a coming together of Church and state in an alliance informed by earlier and pre- Roman views of reality. These attitudes were deeply influential in informing both ecclesiastical and civil attitudes, and legislation for almost the next two millennia.

The prevailing reactions towards suicide deepened over the ensuing centuries. In medieval times the practice of 'punishing' the corpse continued. Courts were held to convict those suspected of killing themselves. The already dead bodies of those convicted were often hung head down from gibbets in public squares; they could only be removed from their homes through upper windows or through holes excavated under the door thresholds, underlining the dread in which the bodies were still held. Burials if they took place at all, were outside consecrated ground – often at crossroads and sometimes with a stake through the heart. Alternatively, bodies were dumped instead in sewers or on rubbish heaps. These practices are deeply reminiscent of earlier tribal attitudes and appear to echo the same fear and horror in a remarkably similar way. Gradually, however, to these rituals and to the stigma that they implied for families, was added a more sinister note that involved the confiscation of the goods and property of the deceased, thus rendering dependants penniless and frequently without even a roof over their heads. The web of punishment was broadening. A famous French eighteenth-century engraving entitled 'The Desecration of the Corpse' depicts the naked corpse of a young man being dragged through the streets behind a horse on the way to the ritual hanging. He has been convicted of the 'crime' of suicide and his widow and small children watch in horror as they await their own fate.

In the nineteenth century attitudes began to change; suicide came to be seen by the emerging influential medical profession as the result of mental illness or insanity. However, this was of little comfort to surviving families; for while their inheritance was generally untouched, they now had to contend with the profound stigma of insanity which was deemed to be hereditary, thus deepening and adding another layer to their experience of marginalisation. In previous years they had had to contend with their deceased loved one being labelled 'bad'; now they were all defined as 'mad' instead, and were shunned and with even greater vigour. Legacies of such attitudes continued well into living memory in Ireland. In some areas a suicide in the family is still something to be hidden and ashamed of. The discovery of the stigma of a suicidal, and hence in community lore, mentally ill, relation – no matter how distant – can still be seen as justifiable reason for preventing a 'good' marriage. The fact that many insurance companies will refuse payment if a death has been defined as suicide also harks back to the punishment of survivors.

The majority churches in Ireland did little to remedy the pain heaped on the heads of bereaved survivors. Folk memory is all too redolent with stories of funerals being turned away from consecrated ground by righteous incumbents. The sad mounds amid the tiny hillocks beyond many rural cemetery walls bear visible and heartrending testimony to the bodies of suicides buried among the remains of unbaptised babies; both excluded in death as often in life. The fact that many clergy would only bury those who had taken their own lives if they were defined as being of 'unsound mind', was of dubious comfort to the grieving family, merely exchanging one stigma for a worse one.

Up until 1961 suicide was still a criminal offence in Northern Ireland. It is only in 1993 that suicide was decriminalised in the Republic of Ireland. Prior to these dates, to take one's own life was a criminal offence in both legislatures, and those who attempted it could, at least in theory, be charged with a crime. A powerful legacy of these realities is still part of our normal speech; we speak still of 'committing' suicide, a term normally only associated with a crime. In linking this use of words to the act of suicide we make a powerful and often deeply hurtful statement about those who take their own life. It is little wonder that families sought to hide the facts and that charitably disposed coroners often found ways around giving the verdict of suicide, lest the full punitive rigours of State, Church and community descend upon the heads of the bereaved.

Survivors of other forms of death have at least been able to depend on the support of time honoured rituals of Church and community. These conveyed a sense of solidarity and care, and a reinforcement of the norms of belief. Instead, for thousands of years those bereaved by suicide have in the main been ignored and marginalised, forced to bear their grief, guilt, anger and pain in a silence that compounded their loss. Many of those whose stories appear in this collection bear witness to the fact that such attitudes are far from dead in our twenty-first century society. Social marginalisation, lack of support and isolation may well be significant factors in the ending of life by suicide; many of those who are bereaved by suicide attest to the significance of such factors as they seek to come to terms with their loss. Such is the power of malign history.

As with many facets of Irish life, James Joyce in Ulysses summarises much of what we have been saying. Leopold Bloom is on his way to a funeral with two companions:

*'But worst of all,'* Mr. Power said, *'is the man who takes his own life. The greatest disgrace to have in the family'*

*'Temporary insanity, of course,'* Martin Cunningham said decisively. *'We must take the charitable view.'*

## 1.3    Societal Context

Significant commentators suggest that Irish society is in a state of flux; many core values and structures are changing; new ones have not yet evolved to take their place. Coupled with this there continues to be a significant legacy of negativity that results in the marginalisation of both those who are suicidal and those who have been bereaved by suicide.

The certainties of life, clear patterns of normative behaviour, and individuals' expectations of what is possible or desirable have changed dramatically and in a relatively short time. Political, social and religious structures have not yet caught up with these trends and frequently find themselves in disarray, either seeking to retrench into old customs or shibboleths, or floundering for footholds in the flood of new thinking and new dreams.

Irish society is seen by sociologists and anthropologists as being in that transitional phase where time honoured values, structures and practices either do not have the same effectiveness as in the past, or are experienced as redundant or meaningless. As yet clear alternatives have not emerged; it is both an exciting and a deeply perturbing era in which to live. Pressures are great and the individual can frequently feel alone and lost without the former physical and ideological norms and structures which, though often resented, provided security and predictability.

While societies are in a transitional phase and much is fluid and in process, there are still bedrock values and prejudices that remain influential. These are often held at a semi-conscious level of awareness within society and tend to be maintained by the power groupings and the majorities in a culture. Those who become most aware of them are those who transgress such deeply held positions.

The demise of many social structures together with the maintenance of subtle and powerful pressures to conform create many sites of vulnerability and powerlessness in our society. In such a context, individuals or groupings who find themselves at the margins of society, because they do not conform or 'fit' in some way, are most vulnerable to the processes of shunning that they encounter. They are made acutely aware by the wider society of their inability or unwillingness to conform. Sometimes the pain and aloneness of their position becomes unbearable.

Suicide occurs for a complex range of reasons one of which may be poor mental health. However, to say that an individual takes their life only when mentally ill or depressed, as has at times been advanced, is at best an over simplification. It is also important to recognise that where mental illness exists, this may well be a reaction to the individual's life experiences such as poverty, lack of vocational opportunity and the breakdown of support systems. If we content ourselves with seeing suicide as solely an outcome of mental ill-health, or viewing mental ill-health as being unrelated to wider societal issues, we will look no further for causes and will ignore the possibility that there are also significant social, cultural, individual and political factors at play. We do not know why many people decide to end their lives. Reductionist statements focusing purely on issues of mental health tend to obscure other significant factors, as well as creating a limited field for analysis and exploration. A much more valid approach is to suggest that the phenomenon of suicide (or indeed mental health) can only be validly analysed through much wider frames of reference.

In any act with suicidal intent there tends to be an intricate web of factors at work, having their roots in the inter-related areas of political, cultural, and individual contexts.

## 1.4 Political, Cultural and Individual Issues

Political ideologies and decisions affect everyday living in significant ways. Early feminist theorists state that the personal is political, suggesting that our actions and thinking take place within political contexts. Political decisions are often based in ideological positions and power drives that may have little to do with local priorities or constituents' everyday needs or realities. Decisions having profound effects on the quality of individual or community living are regularly made with little reference to local needs. These decisions are often quite arbitrary in that they support or privilege certain groupings and communities while marginalising and oppressing others. Many inner-city urban areas exist where unemployment is high, educational and development resources are under-funded and problems are rife. Significant numbers are caught in poverty traps with little hope of change. In rural areas a different set of political and economic agendas have created situations where quality of life and opportunity is equally compromised. In both contexts the rate of suicide is significantly higher than in privileged middle class suburban areas.

Politics and culture are closely related to each other as well as to the experience of living. A society's culture is formed by among other things, a distillation of its history, popular temperament, demographic trends, religion and geography. Societal organisation and the aspirations of the dominant groupings are also important in its make-up. Culture is not passive and is in a process of evolution and change over time. Every society has particular cultural norms that it honours and privileges over others;

both explicit and implicit priorities and values are rooted in this process. In every culture there are the dominant groupings that conform to these as well as sub-groupings that to a greater or lesser extent reflect a different range of values and practices. In the recent past for instance southern Irish culture honoured nationalism, the norms of conservative Catholicism, rural lifestyle values, and a somewhat ambivalent attitude towards law and order. A different set of values, rooted in a different cultural heritage, obtained in Northern Ireland. In the last decade or so the dominant cultures, and hence the accepted values, both North and South, have changed; both now increasingly value wealth over community service, religion plays a less central part in determining values, work role tends to define identity and financial success is central.

In the past an individual could obtain status and a sense of significance because of their role in the local community or indeed by being a caring and responsible parent, spouse or sibling. Life worth is now measured increasingly in more monetary terms, or in terms of connection with the moneyed and powerful. Those who cannot, or who choose not to conform to the values of the developing culture come to occupy positions of increasing marginality. Their voices tend to go unheard. The significance of community and family has come to mean less and less and the supports once offered by local social structures are becoming increasingly diluted. Researchers suggest that those who choose suicide as their option have frequently experienced a sense of disconnectedness from their community, its supports and its values. They may also belong to groups who are either explicitly or implicitly marginalised within the culture and society.

Trends within recent suicide figures suggest that certain groupings within society are particularly vulnerable. The suicide rates for men, particularly young men and those living in rural areas, have increased dramatically in recent years. A number of hypotheses have been advanced to explain this phenomenon. Firstly young men in particular exist in a social context where there is a lot of uncertainty about role and identity. Many of the old models for acceptable male behaviour have been discredited. In the recent past what tended to be valued in men was physical strength, a lack of emotion, dominant behaviour and a commitment to work outside the home. What is now expected is much less clear and many men feel vaguely that they are expected to be supporters, carers, and emotional resources as well as being strong and dominant providers.

This lack of clarity and sense of demand places a huge strain on younger men as they seek for relevant role models and acceptable expressions of masculinity. Many men are also increasingly isolated within lifestyles that are highly competitive and stressful. Few men have been brought up to recognise or share their emotional pain and few contexts exist in which they can do so. The club, the pub, the church, the gym, the work place or the street corner do not easily facilitate this. Secondly, men in deprived areas, in conjunction with the rest of such populations, experience high levels of financial, educational and vocational choice deprivation with a reduced number of the informal social supports than might have existed in the past.

For young men in rural occupations, particularly farming, the life style is increasingly socially isolated and much more demanding than in the past. The demand for increased acreage and longer and longer working hours to maintain economic viability, fewer and fewer people working larger and larger tracts of land, and the drain of population from the countryside, make for lifestyles that are increasingly isolated and unsustainable. A bachelor farmer living alone and working the land inherited from a line of forebears, and experiencing the pressures of the catastrophic plunge in the price of lamb and other results of decisions made far away in Brussels may find it easier to end his own life rather than facing what appears to be social disgrace, public bankruptcy and the sense of failing past generations. The fact that he is part of a social structure that does not easily facilitate marriage or companionship and a culture that accepts alcohol abuse as normal may also be of some considerable relevance. It is not possible to make sense of his suicide without looking at the wider political and cultural realities that formed the background of his life.

The rate of women's suicide is highest among homemakers. In exploring this figure it is necessary to acknowledge the political and cultural backdrop that undervalues this highly central role in our society, allowing it to go unacknowledged and financially unrewarded. Many women speak of the social and financial pressures that force them to work as well as rearing a family and the difficulty of balancing home commitments and outside employment. This is in itself an indicator that at some levels the traditional values of male dominance and patriarchy are still alive and well in our culture, despite cosmetic changes.

A figure that sometimes causes surprise is the relatively high rate of suicide among the elderly. This trend is observable in almost every country of the European Union. Many older people speak of the difficulty of finding meaningful roles in life following retirement. For men, whose sense of identity and self worth has been tied to employment this may be a particularly significant reality. Others speak of the painful discovery that the roles that they occupy in family or community are, due to changes in society, no longer valued or recognised. Due to increasing mobility among younger people many grandparents find they have little connection with their grandchildren; they can no longer fulfil the role of significant carers. Organisations that were central to community well-being are finding it increasingly difficult to maintain their work because younger people no longer have the time or commitment to service them. This has two consequences for the elderly. Firstly, these organisations were frequently central to maintaining a cohesive community where people knew each other and where the needs of young and old were recognised and met. Without cohesion, community becomes a meaningless concept characterised by loneliness and isolation. Secondly, many people who gave large amounts of time and talent to such organisations now face the pain of watching these organisations and their own role within them disintegrate.

Recent research suggests that elderly suicide rates are high where there is a lack of real social support, particularly in times of illness. The concept of community care is admirable, where elderly people can remain at home supported by a range of well resourced services attending to physical, psychological and emotional needs and in a context that makes life not just comfortable but meaningful. Too often, however, it has meant, in practice, elderly people abandoned to sketchy and under-resourced services, cared for by over stretched professionals or family members. Such older people facing illness, loneliness, a sense of diminished personal significance and the prospect of becoming a burden on overstretched resources may well become minded to consider suicide as an option.

A young gay man who takes his own life because he cannot cope with the isolation of his experience, and the attitude of Church and community to his situation, does not make this choice purely because he is depressed. He may be so, but that depression cannot be seen in isolation but rather as the outcome of experiences of marginalisation, taunting by school peers, and his sense of rejection by his church. The man whose business or farm has 'failed', or the pupil who does not get acceptable marks in exams, is confronting a deeply held societal value that defines both success and failure in very narrow terms. The reactions encountered are attributable to the culture of our society that accepts, labels, rejects, and scapegoats. It is significant to note that alcohol and substance misuse show a positive co-relation with both mental ill-health and with suicide. Both also tend to be particularly prevalent in socially deprived areas where they are associated with poverty and lack of educational or vocational opportunity, and the breakdown of family and community structures.

Suicide in our culture has long been associated with the idea of lack of meaning, or with restricted options. From Durkheim onwards, researchers and theorists have suggested that those who find that their ways of making sense of the world or of life events has been undermined are more susceptible to suicidal thinking. George Kelly, the American philosopher/psychologist, suggests that suicide tends to take place when the individual feels themselves to be without meaningful support and with very few alternatives that make any sense. Other theorists would agree. Life has become too difficult or two painful. Death is not seen as necessarily desirable in itself, but as a way of stopping the pain which has become unbearable.

The individual's experience of life is significantly influenced by both the political and cultural realities of society as well as by gene make up, mental and physical resources, particular family dynamic, history of difficult or fulfilling life events, as well as general outlook and disposition. Each of us is actively involved in conjunction with external realities in weaving our own way of making sense of the events of our life and developing our value systems, our sense of purpose, identity and meaning in life. The values that are central in our society and in our community, together with the particular range of experiences that an individual has been exposed to, are very significant in creating the contexts in which we live. They create the range opportunities and strictures

FROM DESPAIR TO HOPE

through which we learn to value ourselves and interpret our experience of living. They create the templates through which we experience and measure our quality of life. They largely define the choices and opportunities that we feel able or unable to make; they define what is acceptable in society. The individual's particular experience of living, the life events that they have encountered, their family background, their ability to cope with crisis, their previous exposure to suicide and their mental health, these are all important variables in the complex process that promotes or reduces the likelihood of suicide. In the last analysis a sustainable and caring society that promotes equality of opportunity, tolerance of difference and recognises the varying needs of its constituent groupings, promotes lives that are themselves sustainable and worthwhile.

Political, social and cultural influences; experiences of deprivation or marginalisation; pressure without adequate support; personal history; all these combine to create the backdrop for acts of attempted or successful suicide. Such acts make sense and have meaning at both individual and societal levels. As Christians our analysis and responses to suicide will be fundamentally flawed if we do not attend both to individual issues at a psychological and pastoral level as well as to the political, sociological and ideological issues that make life for some unbearable or unsupportable.

## 1.5    The Role of the Churches

The followers of Jesus Christ are variously exhorted to be lights in the world, or yeast in the dough, or more specifically still, to be transformers of society rather than being conformed to its existing values. It is a sad reality that in suicide as in many other areas, the churches have lagged . far behind progressive social attitudes. Historically, with few exceptions the churches have reflected and reinforced society's negative attitude to the suicidal and to those they left behind. More frequently churches were in the vanguard, adding significantly to the layers of pain, guilt and ostracisation experienced.

Churchgoers, with few exceptions, tend to be one of the most conservative groupings in society. Perhaps churches have become refuges for those who are frightened by change rather than contexts in which those who are seeking to be catalysts for change, for justice and for freedom find support and inspiration.

This is not and need not be the whole picture. In some quarters there exists a truly radical vision of what it is to be followers of Jesus at the beginning of the twenty-first century. There is also huge potential for change. The churches represent one of the largest groupings in Irish society and have considerable influence at their disposal that can be used to bring about social and political change. They also have vast resources, particularly in the realm of personnel, relevant experience, skill-base, and often good-will that can be mobilised to support those who are in difficulty. Churches at their best also demonstrate the value of true community, offering care, acceptance, inclusion and dynamic love. Many outstanding individual believers and groups of believers illustrate this.

In responding to the challenge of suicide it is important to concentrate our energies in at least three specific areas.

*Pastoral*
Irish religious society has tended for historical reasons to be highly minister or priest centred. While Evangelical Non-conformity has in principle opposed this position, in practice the differences have been tokenistic rather than real. Many of the newer churches have been far more radical in their practice of 'body ministry' and in the exemplification of the priesthood and ministry of all believers. These principles imply the recognition that every individual as well as sub grouping in the Church has

a particular range of gifts and ministries that it is the duty of the Church to recognise and develop.

Pastoral care is a very central ministry for the development of a healthy Church or community. At its best it facilitates the expression and integration of emotional and psychological pain. It nurtures healing. It also recognises that there is a societal as well as an individual context to both pain and healing. Such pastoral care comes naturally to only very few; on the other hand there are not many who cannot learn the primary skills of empathy, authenticity and sensitive listening that are required.

Too often this is an area that has been the Cinderella of Church training programmes. Ministerial education has tended to occupy itself more with exegetical or liturgical niceties rather than the development of skills that enable the recognition of and intervention in human pain. This must be changed. Ministers, leaders, youth leaders and ordinary Church members need to be offered contexts in which the skills of radical caring can be developed. Only then will the pain of the suicidal or those bereaved through suicide be attended to in or through the church. Only then will it be possible for the Church to become a healing influence in society or in its local community.

### Community

A sense of disconnection or rootlessness is thought by many researchers to lie at the base of suicide. Churches have at their centre the ideal of dynamic living community where the individual finds love, challenge, acceptance and significance; a place where their uniqueness is both recognised and reverenced. Often the reality is very different and worship, structure and attitudes are experienced as marginalising and irrelevant to all but a cosy in-group. Developing a local church life that is vibrant and inclusive of young, middle-aged and old, that respects difference and that reflects unconditional love is not easy. However, the literature, philosophy and practice of community development theorists and practitioners, not to mention New Testament models, offer a huge range of relevant material that can be of use in the creation and support of such lively, nurturing and spiritually alive communities. Theorists and practitioners in the fields of organisational dynamics and the developing area of leadership theory will also provide useful resources.

Again many of the newer Pentecostal style churches have developed styles of worship that are exciting and dynamic involving huge numbers of both old and young people in meaningful community spirituality. The quality of what is on offer in many churches is so poor and threadbare as to alienate all but the most loyal faithful. People vote with their feet and rather than bemoan empty pews it is more useful to respond creatively and prayerfully to the challenge that they pose. In this process of developing creative and inclusive worship, it is not a matter of 'either or' but 'both and', where the best of contemporary and traditional are brought together. Often it is not the content of the Christian message that is experienced as unattractive but the threadbare packaging in which it has been presented.

Creating dynamic worship will not, however, guarantee a relevant connection with people; it must be the outcome of a leadership that is deeply spiritually committed as well as sensitive to and aware of the trends and issues of today's society. This must also go hand in hand with an inclusive and respectful attitude to those whose life-styles are less conformist.

The nurturing of such community life takes vision and a leadership that is both open and unafraid to risk. It also suggests a style of leadership that is facilitative and inclusive rather than domineering and directive. And it suggests leaders who are able to be personally vulnerable and in touch with their own pain. Above all it takes a willingness to change. Frequently we have the seeds of possibility in our local churches; these, however, need to be honed and refined and opened to the movements of the Holy Spirit in an exciting journey of growth and development.

*Critical reflection*

Prevailing culture, societal norms and expectations, and political decision making are seen as significant factors in rising suicide rates. Observing, analysing, critiquing and commenting upon these areas is central to the church's role if it is to be a change agent in society. The Apostle Paul challenges Christians not to be conformers. Down the centuries individual believers have banded together to challenge the status quo and to create social and political change where there has been injustice or structural sin in society. They have also become engaged in creating internal change where there has been abuse or bad practice within the church's own ranks.

When the church, irrespective of denomination, has been at its healthiest, it has sought to alter the prevailing culture and the political status quo and to adopt the role of change agent where this has been necessary rather than being tamed to become the handmaid of society's power groupings. At other times the Church has adopted the more passive role of conforming to prevailing cultural and political norms and there has been an unquestioning acceptance of certain practices and a reluctance to critique or threaten internal or external power-bases. This is illustrated on the one hand by all but a minority of the German churches' quiet acceptance of the prevailing attitudes of Nazi philosophy in the pre-World War II era. It has also been prevalent in the Irish Roman Catholic Church's more recent tendency to ignore the issue of child sexual abuse when it first arose among its clergy. An unquestioning attitude allows such possibilities to go unchecked.

To become healthy and to have a significant part in creating or sustaining a fair and just society that meets the social, psychological, educational and emotional needs of individuals, families and communities, the Church must develop and nurture its critical faculties. In doing so it must both look inwards to critique its own structure and practices and look outward to comment on and mobilise change in the wider socio-political arena.

In order to achieve this, the raising of awareness among ministers, leaders and those at grassroots must be attended to. Training programmes, sermons as well as the agendas of synods and other meetings must prioritise the art and discipline of social analysis and comment.

Suicide is a real and uncomfortable reality in our society. For many it is heartbreakingly so. The time has come to address the issues that it calls our attention to. The Church does not have any monopoly here; it does, however, have an important role to fulfil with other agencies in society. The recent Government Task Force Report emphasises the need for co-operation of all those agencies who are concerned in the area; working co-operatively much can be achieved.

## 1.6    Some myths about suicide

There is some confusion about what is fact and what is fiction around the issue of suicide. It is useful to unpack fact from fiction in the myths.

| Fiction | Fact |
| --- | --- |
| When people begin to improve following a crisis, then the suicide risk is over | Suicide often occurs when a person's situation improves. Then they possess the energy and will to turn their negative automatic thoughts into self-destructive actions |

| Fiction | Fact |
|---|---|
| Suicidal behaviour is a sign of mental illness | Suicidal behaviour indicates deep unhappiness and a high level of hopelessness, but not necessarily mental illness |
| Suicide occurs in certain groups only – rich/poor, young/old | Suicide occurs in all groups in society |
| You are either the suicidal type or not | It could happen to anyone |
| Those who talk about it are least likely to attempt it | Most people who have died by suicide have talked to others about it in the recent past |
| Getting a person to open up and talk about suicide encourages it | Giving a person time and space to talk about how they are feeling may offer them hope |
| It is mostly females who are a high suicide risk | Young men in the 15 to 24 age group are at the highest risk, with a ratio of three males to one female |
| Suicide happens without warning | Suicidal people often give indications by their actions or words beforehand |

# PERSONAL STORIES

## 2.1    Introduction

Each of the stories* in this section will be followed by a
brief reflection. The purpose of each reflection will be to
weave together some of the threads of the story and some
of the insights of the Christian tradition, and to do this in
a way that will be helpful for Christian people who are
confronting the reality of suicide.

The Church is called, at all times, to ongoing reflection
on its faith and its life, in light of the grace of God in Jesus
Christ. And yet the most lasting and valuable of these
reflections are often those that are shaped during times of
vulnerability and fragility in the Church's life.

In particular, when we have to face the reality of
suicide, either in the wider community or among our

---

\*    The names used in these stories are not the real names of the people
concerned. The events themselves, however, are real – some as
described, some are composed from a number of real experiences.

Christian neighbours, our self-understanding, our assumptions about the world, and even our faith may be called profoundly into question. These stories of suicide thus invite us to reflect not only on issues of bereavement and pastoral care, but also on the Church's very life and self-understanding.

The purpose of these reflections, therefore, is not to suggest specific pastoral responses to the situations described. Such suggestions can be found elsewhere in this booklet. Here we want only to ask: Can each of these painful human stories of despair and loss become a mirror held up to our sight as Christian churches? And if we look clear-eyed into the mirror, what do we see?

## 2.2   Mary's Story

*The final tragedy of an elderly woman whose lifestyle was not perceived as isolated*

Mary was aged 66, and she had been a widow for four years. She had one daughter, living in the west, while the eldest son, with his wife and three children, live in the family home. There were two other sons, living in England.

She lived at home, with farming parents, and worked locally, until her marriage at age 24 years. Her husband was a substantial farmer, the family were well respected locally and had friends in the neighbourhood. On the death of her husband, the farm was willed to the eldest son, with provision for a cash payment to each of the other children and Mary was given residential rights in the family home for her life. On assuming the ownership of the family farm, the eldest son and his family returned to live in the family home from a cottage on the edge of the farm.

Mary was dependent on her son for pocket money and other necessary expenses. She had to ask for money when she needed it and there was little understanding of her need for independence. She was dependent on her family to take her shopping, for social outings and to attend church. At first these were regular outings, but later they became infrequent.

The family home is a large house, needing renovation, but is reasonably comfortable with good facilities. She had meals with the family, had her own bedroom and shared the bathroom facilities. She did not feel free to invite friends to call and their visits became infrequent and stopped altogether. Some months later tensions began to mount – sharing the kitchen was difficult and Mary did not feel welcome in the family room. She spent more and more time in her room, taking meals with her. It was inadequately heated and had no television.

All this increased her sense of isolation and loneliness. She spent long hours alone and developed health problems. She was breathless after climbing stairs, and her spirits were low. Sleep was poor.

A routine visit to her GP raised his concerns and she was referred for psychiatric and medical reports. She was found to have a depressive illness and some heart and arthritis problems. A conference was held with her family, who had little insight into why she was depressed. Mary suggested that she move to live in the farm cottage and a granddaughter offered to sleep with her. Although not ideal this was agreed to, with a promise of home support from the health professionals. Her daughter was doubtful, but was not offering any other solution.

Initially, this worked well. Mary improved, having a sense of belonging in her new home and her sense of independence was restored.

The grandchildren left home some months later. She was not eating properly, failing to take medication and complaining of being lonely and sad, with breathlessness and joint pains that meant she was becoming housebound. The visiting nurse detected depression and malnutrition. Mary's concentration and interest were poor. She was withdrawn and admitted she had lost her sense of 'God in her life'. Further support measures were put in place, with

FROM DESPAIR TO HOPE

limited success. A return to the family home seemed not to be an option.

Some weeks later a family member called, but she was not there. A search revealed that she was in the river. She did not respond to resuscitation. Death was due to drowning – she probably died by suicide.

Shock and distress with guilt feelings followed for the family who all needed counselling and pastoral care for some time. Even now, their understanding of what happened is incomplete.

*Discussion and reflection*
Sometimes one of the hardest things for committed Christian people to come to terms with is the experience of having done your best for someone else, having tried to help another person, having acted with good intentions, and then having to face the fact that instead of doing good, you ended up doing damage.

Christian teachers have helped us to reflect on this difficult and painful experience by pointing out that human sinfulness can become visible not only in people's personal choices, but also in human social structures. This 'structural sin' means that sometimes good intentions are not enough. Sometimes the structures of society, family, education, or Church may be set up in such a way that the well-meaning actions of people within them still end up having sinful and damaging effects. And when this happens, it may be more helpful to re-examine the structures themselves than to blame individuals for the results of their behaviour.

One way of understanding Mary's story is to suggest that she was the unintended victim of a whole set of structures and assumptions that governed both family life and rural culture. These assumptions functioned throughout her life to increase her vulnerability and to deprive her of an appropriate level of self-determination within her marriage, family, and community.

For example, Mary never lived independently, but always in a home seen to belong ultimately to someone else. The accepted patriarchal inheritance structure left Mary with little provision for herself, and perhaps did not recognise sufficiently the extent to which she had been a partner in the farming enterprise all her working life. She had no financial independence after her husband's death, and no mobility. In a sense, she was returned to the status of a child after her husband's death, completely dependent on others, and denied the means by which she might maintain and develop adult friendships in the community.

In some ways it was no wonder that Mary developed health problems, as her various ailments only reflected the invalidity that had already been imposed upon her. It is perhaps also no wonder that Mary claimed to have lost the sense of God in her life, since her own sense of adult dignity, her sense of herself as a person who needs others but who also has much to give to others, was being systematically undermined.

It is almost certainly the case that neither Mary's husband nor any of her children ever meant her harm, or ever made any decisions concerning her with destructive intent. Nevertheless, the collective impact of the assumptions they made (and perhaps Mary made them as well) was to systematically diminish her selfhood and increase her vulnerability to dangerous levels. And rather than pointing the finger of blame at individuals, it may be more helpful to re-examine the assumptions under which all the members of Mary's family operated.

In his teaching to the disciples, Jesus implied that faithfulness to the gospel would shake up many unquestioned loyalties and assumptions where family structures are concerned. Indeed, one of the most frequent criticisms of the Christian Church in the first centuries of its existence was that it undermined rigid patriarchal family structures.

## 2.2   Teenage Addiction

*Suicide in the context of inner city social deprivation. A letter found in the jacket of an eighteen year-old who was discovered dead following a heroin overdose in an East Belfast flat*

Mum,

I hate writing this, but I have to, to try to explain. It's going to be shite for you and Fiona getting it; she's a great wee sister, tell her.

It's all a bit clearer now since you made me go to that addiction group. That gave me a handle on what's been going on for me – it kinda gives you a bit of control if you understand. I guess that's why I'm writing this too. I think it really started when Dad left, there was all the rows first and then suddenly he'd gone. Every one kept telling me to be strong and that I was a man and I'd have to look after you both. Or else they said nothing and just looked at me – like there was something wrong with me. I didn't know what to do. I was only ten. I really hate that f***** for what he did to us. He still messes my head, ringing and texting me – saying he wants to see me or he's worried about me, and then doesn't ring again for months or send me the fare or anything. He doesn't care, all he cares about are his new family. I really hate him.

School was a real mess – it was so boring; they used to make a fool out of me if I asked questions. But we got our own back – Macca and me made two teachers cry in the class and we gave that new teacher a breakdown, they didn't mess with us again. Mr Wilson was the only one who was any good, he kinda understood, said I was real bright, it was just school didn't stretch me enough. Said the school system was failing me and I wasn't the failure. I really liked history when he taught it. But then he left.

That's when Jimmy got me in with the paras – it was deadly – all the young kids were afraid of me. I got to know why we had to hate the Taigues, like it was survival, them or us. Something important to fight for. Big Jimmy said I'd go far, I had what it took – maybe I'd get into the explosives unit. But then the politicians made the peace process and it all fell apart. That's when we all moved onto the hard stuff. I know I'm hooked – I've tried to get off, I really have but it's too hard. Anyway what would I do if I did, I'd have no friends, no clan like I have now everywhere, people who understand. No one would give me a job or anything. I'd be no one.

I'm sorry, Mum,

Love,

Billy.

## Discussion and Reflection

In some respects, Billy's story seems to be the one in which it is most clear what went wrong, and who was to blame. To begin with, there was Billy's father, who left the family home when Billy was ten and continued to send mixed and troubling, though infrequent, messages to his son. There were the destructive, unthinking gender stereotypes that bore down on a young and grieving child as he was told by neighbours that he was now a 'man' and somehow responsible for his competent, adult mother and younger sister.

There were the classroom experiences in which a willingness to perfect the fine art of mutual humiliation seemed the only way to survive, for students and teachers alike. There was the one teacher who encouraged and listened, but then he himself moved on. When school became impossible, there were the paramilitaries, who offered at long last a sense of belonging, but one entirely dependent on the continued and unchanging presence of a well-defined enemy. And finally, there was the heroin, which, for a while, helped to dull Billy's terrible sense that his precarious security had been taken from him once again.

In some ways, therefore, this story fits comfortably into the worldview held by many Christians, reinforcing a whole host of negative stereotypes about 'broken' families, lack of discipline in schools, paramilitary involvement, and heroin addiction. The challenge for us who hear Billy's story is, therefore, to try to go beyond these stereotypes, even though they may contain some elements of truth, and ask ourselves some difficult questions about the world in which Billy lives, and the Church's complicity or involvement with that world.

For what is also clear from Billy's story is how much was right and good in his life, as well as how much went wrong. He was a bright and intelligent young man, who led his best teacher to claim that it was the school system, not Billy, that was failing. He had a well-developed ability to empathise with the feelings of others, so that his last act was to try to explain his desperation to his mother and somehow soften the blow that he knew his death would be to her. And finally, he was a young man who never lost his sense of the importance of belonging to a community larger than himself, of being bound to others by ties of friendship, loyalty, and trust. Most congregations would be delighted if all the children they raised showed the same qualities at the age of 18 years!

And yet what Billy needed, and could not find, was a place of belonging and security that at the same time provided him with room to grow and change in response to the changing circumstances around him. What was at the core of Billy's final despair was the recurring fear that there was no other life for him than the one that he had recently found, but which had now fallen apart.

And, therefore, Billy's story offers a particular challenge to all Christians involved in working with young people. And that challenge is to ask ourselves whether or not we are providing a place for young people like Billy to deal with the most fundamental upheavals in their lives, and the most troubling questions, while offering at the same time a steady companionship that masks no hidden agenda of our own, but is grounded in the simple, transparent respect and regard of the gospel.

And at the same time, Billy's story challenges us to clarify what exactly we mean by that often casually used term, 'Christian work'. Maybe if there had been churches in Billy's neighbourhood who had supported a youth programme designed and carried out in partnership with local residents, Billy's life could have been different. On the other hand, however, maybe if the local churches had not insisted on their 'own' programme, but had helped in some way to support the struggling teachers in Billy's school, or the work of the vocational training centre, or some other local or political initiative, Billy's life could also have been different.

Perhaps we all need to exercise greater humility and attention in trying to discern what 'Christian work' might look like in a given setting, and in admitting how diverse the forms of Christian discipleship practised by individuals and congregations may turn out to be. What is certain, however, is that the biblical call to enact social justice for people like Billy is inextricably linked with the longing he experienced for a safe place in which to find room to move and grow into a future in which he would have a place. And it is perhaps no coincidence that one of the oldest biblical images for salvation is precisely that, a place with room to live and breathe and grow.

---

*For Discussion*

As Christians we believe that our baptism serves as our call to discipleship, and yet at the same time, we also believe that this call can take on a wide variety of different forms or expressions at different stages of our lives. How might you explain to an 18 year old like Billy your own ongoing struggle to give shape and form to the calling of your baptism?

---

## 2.4    A Bible Christian
*Suicide resulting from the disappearance of faith structures and the erosion of a particular denominational way of life*

It was a mystery how Jacob discovered that we were Methodists also. But two nights after we arrived at the holiday house he appeared at the back door, red faced, enthusiastic and tongue-tied. Over the next three years in which we spent our summer break in his native village this ritual repeated itself as he spent most evenings with us. At first it was fascinating, listening to the stories of times past, then it became deeply irritating; ultimately as we began to realise the depth of his need for a context in which he felt safe, it became a profound learning experience. Through him we were introduced to the depth of isolation that may at times be experienced in Irish society by those who see themselves as different in a highly homogeneous community.

Even his name singled him out, in a countryside full of Seáns, Paddys, Eddies or even the occasional George. He would speak with delight and enthusiasm of times past when he had been part of a small but vibrant community that had formed, reflected and supported his ethos and identity. He spoke of meetings and fellowship and warmth. Now there was only himself.

The derelict Methodist chapel, in whose fellowship and fear his deep evangelical faith had been formed and where the fervour of generations of his extended family had been nurtured, still stood on the land that he farmed. Emigration, the 'Ne Temere' decree and deep changes in the fabric of Irish society had reduced it from viability to nothingness in less than a generation. On the death of his parents Jacob had become the sole survivor of a distinct ethos and spirituality; and the little chapel was closed – yet another such statistic in the Minutes of the annual Methodist Conference. For Jacob, it was the beginning of the end.

He had drunk deeply not only from the wells of evangelical spirituality, but also from its legalism and negativity. Socialising where there was drinking, dancing or any hint of gambling seemed to him irreconcilable with Christian belief; association with 'the others' particularly with romantic intent was totally taboo. Thus the warmth of the village pub or the social possibilities of Macra na Feirme were seen as forbidden.

Even the occasional Church of Ireland parish hop was seen as suspect. During his parent's lifetime, as the youngest sibling and main carer he had never felt able to follow his brothers and sisters to Dublin, London or

FROM DESPAIR TO HOPE

Melbourne, and now at 52 it seemed just too late. The depth of his aloneness, his sexual frustration, his need for companionship and his deep faith were held in throbbing tension. Once he told me that his only social outlet, to which he looked forward with something like desperation, was an occasional Faith Mission prayer meeting.

After the closure of his chapel he had had occasional visits from the Superintendent of the far flung circuit; perhaps because of distance or because of Jacob's neediness these had ultimately dwindled to nothing. He still made a sixty-five mile round trip every Sunday to sit with four or five others in the damp depression of the nearest Non-conformist cause. He was the youngest by at least twenty years.

The tide of faith and its structures, which had nurtured and formed not just his spirituality but his identity, had receded, leaving him stranded and alone on a cold and inhospitable beach.

Years after we had changed our holiday venue, we heard there had been a shooting 'accident' on Jacob's farm. His faithful sheepdog attracted the attention of neighbours who found his body ironically slumped within the walls of the derelict chapel.

*Discussion and reflection*
Jacob's story is likely to be one of particular pain, and even anger, for those who belong to one of the minority Christian communities in Ireland, and it is important for us to acknowledge that this is so. It would also be easy to point the finger of blame at the lasting effects of the Ne Temere decree, for example, or at the Church bodies who have taken the decisions to close declining congregations over the years.

However, we may also need to reflect on the experience of Christian faith and community that was Jacob's heritage, and to ask ourselves whether or not this heritage, too, let Jacob down.

To a large extent, Jacob's tightly knit evangelical fellowship was his whole life. It provided him with a way of life, a community of support, and a spiritual identity. All of this was good. And yet when the Methodist chapel closed, Jacob was cut off not only from his particular evangelical spirituality, but also from the social and emotional life of the wider community, because his particular faith tradition had given him no way to connect the two.

At the heart of our Christian faith is the incarnation, the experience and conviction that God, in Jesus Christ, came into the world to live among us, and that the presence of the risen Christ continues with us in the power of the Spirit. All human life is made holy in the incarnation, in the sense that there is no part of human life and experience that is out of reach of God's transforming love.

This means that those of us who come from the evangelical tradition may need to ask ourselves if we still see our Christian calling too much in terms of separation from all that is unfamiliar or unsettling to us, or of which we disapprove. Perhaps Jacob's Christian heritage failed him in this sense. Perhaps it did not teach him that baptism into Christ's body offers believers the freedom to move gracefully and with integrity into new contexts when the occasion demands, while remaining rooted in the strengths of their evangelical faith.

For those of us who still belong to vibrant congregations that are not, like Jacob's, in immediate danger of closure, it might be worthwhile to reflect on our own attitudes to change and loss. We might ask, for example, to what extent our own congregational life and spirituality have prepared us only for a future that is familiar and in which things go on in much the same way as we have always known them to do. And we might also ask whether we are prepared, in the confidence of the gospel, to face both change and loss in our Christian lives,

FROM DESPAIR TO HOPE

both when we see them coming and when they are totally unanticipated.

> *For Discussion*
>
> In your congregation, can you talk openly about loss, whether that loss takes the form of a decline in numbers, the winding up of a long and successful (but now dated) programme, or a local community that is changing around you? Can you mark the ending of something good and important with celebration (as did not seem to happen with the closure of the Methodist chapel)? Do you equate endings with failure, or do you believe that endings, even though they be heart-rending, can also clear a new and life-giving way ahead?

## 2.5 To Live is to Work

*When generations of tradition collapse, so does Michael's will to live – can his wife and family survive?*

Michael was happy in his work. His family retail business founded by his great grandfather and built up by his grandfather and father had ensured good homes for their families as well as educational opportunities for their children. The men were the providers and proud of it. They had not sought opulence – comfortable security was sufficient. But they were not prepared for the onset of vast conglomerates spreading like a rash through their country and city – to which Michael's business, along with others, eventually succumbed.

He had always been the boss, but no longer could he control events. Some years later his wife reflected with sadness: 'Like the ship going down, he went with it'. The cheerful husband and father who never appeared depressed, never consulted a doctor and never took a pill for any reason, refused to face reality for exactly one year following the take-over. With the redundancy package, unemployment benefit, plus his wife's earning power, they struggled to maintain their living standard.

Michael's fiftieth birthday came and went. He decided to be self-employed again, choosing to embark on a new line. But as the launch date drew near, he became tense and apprehensive. On Friday a legal hitch occurred, on Saturday he confided in a brother whose son was terminally ill that he wished he could change places with his nephew, and on Sunday night Michael took his own life by hanging.

The legacy left to his family was the struggle in surmounting the stigma, and learning to live with their loss through suicide. In the beginning, numbed by shock and devastation, each one made up their own story, inventing a reason for the unreasonable. Marion, his wife, who had married Michael when she was 18 and he 25, could feel knives right through her cutting her to pieces. She refused medication until she had told the two younger children, aged 12 and 10, which was her most difficult and painful task. The older two aged 22 and 18 were very brave until a polo-neck sweater was requested for their father's body in the mortuary. Their Dad was a shirt and tie man.

The visiting priest was visibly disturbed by their hysterical reaction and rage. Another priest, who was to take the funeral service, said that for Marion there would be no good things for a long time. That day and week she needed the room and the house to be full, with family, friends and neighbours flocking to their home as ointment for the wounds. The Church was packed, Michael had been so liked. Marion thanked each and every one asking how they were. The tape in her mind kept on and on 'How will I repay? They all own a bit of me.'

Many months later – helped by counselling – her anger and fear were permitted to surface and to process. Such a death was alien, didn't happen in her world. She felt shattered and when driving her car she nervously imagined her husband sitting behind her and attempting to choke her. The violence of his death made her question how she had known him closely for so many years yet not known him in his ability to kill, which had now altered and almost wiped out everything. Michael's suicide had broken a taboo; scary, could there be another in the family? The unthinkable had become thinkable. Marion eventually came to acknowledge that there had been some danger signals: Michael, being from a traditional 'family provider' background, saw the end of his business as total loss – no job, no wife, no family; the shame of role reversal – wife going out to work with him staying at home; the 'job for life' was gone, nothing else was sure; identity crisis – voicing to Marion, 'You are strong, I am weak'; personality changes gone down an octave; starting to show anxiety to others where before it would be contained; lost interest in sex and was fading in communication; in the last month he had, on her insistence, visited the doctor but had rejected the antidepressants.

Marion endured and worked through her agony and feelings of guilt plus the haunting horror of Michael's death. The good memories – which were missing – are reclaimed. Five years on, this caring widow now counsels others in similar major crises. She and her family have faced the pain of living and have found that the sun can come out bit by bit from the shadow of suicide.

*Discussion and reflection*
On first reading, Michael's story seems a very familiar one, that of the middle-aged man whose sense of self-worth is almost entirely shaped and confirmed by his paid employment, and who is therefore in danger of losing his very identity when the supportive structures and recognition of the workplace are taken away.

And there is no doubt that such individualistic attitudes to work are both common and, frequently, destructive. If unquestioned, they can entangle both men and women in patterns of family life that are rigidly inflexible, and unsuited to the changing personal and professional circumstances of their lives. If unchallenged, they allow the practices and assumptions of the workplace to remain unchanged. And what is perhaps most worrying, such attitudes subtly prevent people like Michael from seeing and appreciating the wider economic context of his job loss. Instead of seeing the dysfunction and injustice of a system that rewards the pursuit of cheap labour and undermines local employment, a person like Michael sees only his own apparent failure.

For the Christian community, however, Michael and Marion's story raises another, deeper issue. In many respects, theirs was a life always under control, in which they owed nothing to anyone and in which they were in no one's debt. The greatest truth in Michael's life was that hard work, combined with a sense of duty and responsibility to his family that he was proud to embrace, would secure his family's future. He, and they, would be dependent on no one.

And Marion, too, though her role in the family was a different one, embraced this ideal of control in other, less obvious ways. Although she appeared to adjust more readily to the changed financial circumstances of the family than Michael did, her reactions revealed a woman who also believed that this new situation could be fully managed and adequately controlled within the family.

And thus when Michael took his own life, Marion's grief was exacerbated by her shattered sense of her and their ability to manage life in a rational and successful way. She desperately sought 'a reason for the unreasonable', an explanation that would restore order to her life, and she had waking nightmares about her husband's capacity for violence, which seemed to have appeared out of nowhere. Even the support of a wide and sympathetic circle of friends became a burden to her, as she wondered how she would manage to discharge the debt she now felt she owed them.

In many respects, Marion's feeling and reactions were not at all unusual, and we know from her story that she worked through them all with courage, and in a way that has proven to be life-giving for herself and for others. And yet Michael and Marion's story leaves us with an unsettling question about the patterns of our own lives, and about the difficulty we often experience, in the midst of all the necessities of our lives, in letting go of an attitude of control and embracing, instead, an attitude of expectation.

As Christians, we believe that everything we are and everything we have comes from God. And by affirming that God is our only provider, the One from whom all good things come, we are invited both to relinquish a certain control over the circumstances of our lives and to embrace a new sense of joyful expectation. And this attitude of expectation is grounded not in a calculation of what we are owed, but in a conviction of God's generosity, a generosity that does not protect us from all those events that are able to shatter us, but which is itself not overcome by them.

Of course, the bills will still have to be paid, decisions will still have to be taken, and contracts will still have to be signed. Trust in God's faithfulness, whatever else it is, is not a form of opting out of real life.

But at the end of the day, those who are most openly and unashamedly dependent on God's provision will also be those most able to deal with the unexpected job losses, the inexplicable betrayals, and the irrational events that can so shake the foundations of our lives. Not because 'God provides' in some passive or childish sense, but simply in the sense that in a world in which control and calculation can provide no final certainties, a trust in God's generosity, however unanticipated its forms and surprising its timing, will not put us to shame.

And who knows? It may be that the very contours of our lives will then be reshaped not only by the more obvious forms of God's gracious provision, but even more by our very willingness to live in this state of unprotected expectation that is itself a mark of God's claim upon us.

---

*For Discussion*

How might you, your household, and your congregation, move towards a pattern of life that is based less on a need to control the future, and more on a joyful sense of expectation grounded in God's generosity? What would such a pattern of life look like?

---

## 2.6　Eithne's Story

*Suicide in the aftermath of sexual abuse*

Eithne was small, quiet and petite, invariably dressed in pastel colours. She looked depressed, and was so passive and withdrawn that her friends and work colleagues just gave up on her – it was such heavy going.

And then for no reason at all, it seemed, there would be a violent, angry outburst that both shocked and frightened them. Her history of relationships was known to be a disaster area, characterised by a pattern of rushing in, demanding so much, and then taking flight, leaving her partner confused, resentful and frequently in a turmoil of self doubt. On one occasion she told a work colleague that people terrified her, because she just didn't know how to handle them and consequently erected barriers to hide behind. Life seemed a very lonely, arid and frightening experience.

It was known that her parents were alive and that she had two brothers, but seemed to have very little contact with them. In fact the area of family relationships seemed, if anything, more fraught than the area of friendships.

The reality behind Eithne's life and behaviour was simple and not uncommon. When she was six her mother was hospitalised for what turned out to be a long and serious illness; it was then that her father began to come to her bed; at first it seemed just for comfort and then for more. It was to be their little secret he said; she must tell no one. As the youngest and only girl in the family, she had always felt alone and somehow left out. Now suddenly she felt somehow needed and for the first time special, even though she hated what happened in the darkness of the night. Despite her mother's ultimate recovery, the abuse continued until she was twelve. Then after a year's respite her eldest brother took over. And at sixteen she had been raped coming home from a school disco by a friend's brother. She had tried to speak of some of what had been happening to her, but it was before society recognised that such things happened in 'nice, respectable families', and she was dismissed as evil and full of dreadful imaginings. It wasn't until many years later when everything became too much for her and she overdosed, that she was referred to a counsellor and the full story began to emerge.

There were, however, two major problems. Firstly the experience of sexual abuse had been so long term that it had become core to her very identity. Without this way of viewing herself she would, she felt, not exist at all. It was very much a question of the devil you know being better than nothing at all. Secondly, it seemed to Eithne that the only way in which she might be able to move on would be if her father acknowledged what had happened, what he had done to her. If he did not do this, she felt her life could never move beyond the constraints of its present tortured existence.

And then her father died suddenly of a massive coronary while walking the dog. She went through the funeral like an automaton. Her only means of escape, of finding an entry to a new life was gone. Two days later they found her body, an empty bottle of sleeping pills her last companion.

## Discussion and reflection
There are few people, inside or outside the Christian community, whose hearts would not go out to Eithne, and

who would not be horrified at the violence to which she was subjected as she was growing up. And there is little excuse, at the beginning of the twenty-first century, for ignorance on the part of anyone on this island regarding the long-term effects of sexual abuse on victims and their families. At the very least, Eithne's story should lead us to redouble our efforts to ensure that in our congregations, and in our places of work, the highest standards of child protection are upheld.

However, Eithne's particular story, with its devastating ending, raises another question, one that may be among the most important to be faced by Christians at the beginning of this new century. Eithne's story raises the question of how we understand and talk about sin within the Christian community.

If sin is at its heart a failure to live on this created earth as the people God intended us to be, in fruitful relationship with one another and with the God who made us, then it is clear that Eithne bore in herself many of the marks of sin. Her relationships were difficult, her behaviour unpredictable, and her choices often destructive. Her attitudes to the ordinary tasks of daily life were often extreme or inappropriate, ranging from ignorance and terror to resentment and passivity. Most of the time, she was both isolated and unapproachable.

And yet the most fundamental expression of sin in Eithne's life was not to be found in her difficult behaviour and unreasonable demands. Rather it was to be found, primarily and unequivocally, in the wrong that had been systematically done to her, in the violation of her personal and bodily integrity in ways that would shape her for the rest of her life.

It is true, of course, that having been so profoundly and repeatedly violated, Eithne herself ended up deformed by sin in all the various ways we have seen. This is not, however, to suggest that Eithne was in any way to blame for what had happened to her. On the contrary, she had been doubly sinned against, both when she suffered repeated sexual abuse, and when her first tentative efforts to speak the truth about her experience were dismissed and refused a hearing.

And for precisely this reason it is not difficult to see how much familiar Christian language about sin would neither have made sense nor been helpful to Eithne. So often sin is spoken about in our churches as a kind of fundamental human arrogance and pride, which destroys everything in the path of its own self-aggrandisement and, finally, puts itself in the place of God.

There is no doubt that such a definition describes one very real manifestation of sin, particularly common among those who hold social and economic power. But one of the most profound and helpful insights of feminist theology has been to point out that for many people, and in particular for women like Eithne, sin takes very different forms. If Eithne's life cannot be said to have been the life God intended for her, surely this was not because she suffered from an overbearing arrogance, but rather because of the profound injustice that was done to her, and whose effects continued to shape her life in destructive ways.

Her greatest sin, to put it another way, was not self-promotion, but the passivity in which she still remained trapped, years after the sexual abuse took place. Again, this is not in any way to suggest that Eithne herself was to blame for her situation. But it is to suggest that if the Church's preaching relentlessly personalises sin and simply urges people like Eithne to repent for their own destructive behaviour, without acknowledging in any way the wider context in which they struggle with such behaviour, then a second form of abuse will have been added to the first.

What Eithne needed to hear in her deepest self was that the truest thing about her was not the abuse she suffered and the scars she carried but the worth and promise she continued to bear in God's sight. And only when she had begun to glimpse this truth could Eithne have actually begun to take responsibility for her situation as it now stood, past, present, and future.

---

*For Discussion*

Christian teachers over many centuries have claimed that self-knowledge and knowledge of God always go together, in other words, that if you grow in one, you grow in the other. In your experience, has the Church's preaching and teaching about sin helped or hindered you in coming to understand yourself more clearly and honestly, and in coming to know God more deeply?

---

## 2.7 A Farmer's Story

*Liam recalls his cry for help when his life was all struggle and little meaning*

I am 26 years old. My story is probably not unique, but it seemed to be happening only to me. I felt there was no one to talk to. I am the eldest of three boys and one girl, the assumed successor to the family farm. I completed school with good results and with enough points to go to college: I chose agricultural college and on completion I returned to work on the family farm with my father. My brothers and sister went to college and settled in jobs with good conditions and prospects. They bought cars and could afford holidays abroad.

My life developed into long hours on the farm, meetings with Macra na Feirme, where I met other farmers who lived much as I did, and attendance at church when I could, but it was expected of me. Its only meaning for me was being off the farm and meeting with the local youth club. Free time for us all was limited and spending money was small. I could use the family car when no one else needed it. My sister's friend, Kate, was a college student.

We were attracted and met on her weekends home. She completed her degree and got a good job in Cork. Letters were frequent, then occasional, finally she told me she had met someone else. That hurt – a lot.

My father was set in his ways and did not understand my anxiety to develop the farm and bring in new ideas. Gradually he left more and more work to me, but with no responsibility for financial policy. Farming was in decline – papers, media and friends talked of little else but problems; poor prices, BSE, the pig industry, rain and floods.

I became angry with my father, resentful of my siblings and irritable with my mother. I was not good company and stopped going out. I became depressed and lost interest in the farm. Why was my life so hard compared with my brothers and sister? I could not sleep and got up tired and with little energy. There seemed to be no way out, no one understood and now I did not care either. Life was like a deep black hole, I just wanted to sleep forever.

After a worse than usual row about the need to buy a new tractor, I felt totally alone and hopeless. Then I thought about my mother's tablets; I knew where she kept them. I took enough to make me sleep, my last thoughts were that I had no hope for a future.

My sister found me and raised the alarm. I woke, disappointed and angry to be alive. Gradually I responded, my family slowly came to understand and the health professionals were supportive to us all. A family conference brought problems into the open and some positive decisions were taken for me and to improve farming practice and policy at home. My brothers offered to make it possible for us to employ relief milkers once a month, funds were found to buy me a car. To my surprise, the young people from the church youth group visited and my minister found time to listen, even though he had no farming background. He knew about people.

There are still problems, but I have found friends among farmers and in the church. Farming is not and never will be easy, but I have learnt that I love the land and that this is where I want to be.

*Discussion and reflection*

In many respects, what is most memorable about Liam's story is that it is so unremarkable. As Liam himself says, 'My story is probably not unique'. And indeed, while sympathising with the very real hurt, loneliness, and despair that Liam describes, most of us would hakve to admit to a degree of personal familiarity, in one form or another, with many of the problems Liam faced. Who among us, after all, has never had to worry over uncertain employment prospects, or has never been wounded by the involuntary ending of an important relationship?

And it is for precisely this reason that Liam's story presents us with an uncomfortable question. And that question is simply this: in the midst of the various ongoing struggles of daily life, which are no less difficult for being perfectly ordinary, why is it so hard, and not least in the Christian community, to ask one another for help? Why must we so often require a gesture of despair as the necessary permission to seek another way forward?

At the heart of our faith is a God whose character it is to make out of a place of hopelessness a way of hope for those whom God loves. And there is a sense in which Liam's very gesture of hopelessness was a last, desperate cry for hope, a cry that another way might somehow, and against all the evidence, be opened up before him. In choosing not to go on, Liam expressed his last and most deeply buried longing that a way to go on might yet be found, and that the problems he faced might not be insurmountable after all.

And if we reflect on Liam's story in this way, two further insights suggest themselves. The first is that a choice is never a choice unless there is an alternative. In a way, Liam had to know that he could choose not to go on in order to discover, as he later admitted, that 'I love the land and that this is where I want to be.' This sense of alternatives is often what makes a way forward possible. And yet, the only alternative that Liam could see was simply to give up in despair.

One might reasonably ask, therefore, what role the local church might have played not just as a focus of social activity but also as a place in which the very real problems faced by young farmers in a time of transition might have been usefully discussed, precisely in light of the presence of a God whose character it is to make a way where there is no way, and whose commitment to the created earth and its people is unyielding.

And yet Liam's own story suggests that if the local church is to become such a place, for young farmers like Liam or for any of the rest of us who struggle with the ordinary yet sometimes overwhelming problems of daily life, it is not likely to happen simply as a result of new programmes being put in place. It is much more likely to happen because someone like Liam, or like you, or like me, finds the courage to admit that we are struggling, and to believe that there will be more strength, as the gospel defines strength, in mutual vulnerability than there will ever be in stubborn self-containment.

For when Liam's despair finally comes out into the open, not only is a way forward found for him, but suddenly it is possible, even necessary, for other family members and friends to look at their own assumptions, and at the effects their choices have had on one another's lives. And thus when Liam finally admits to the truth of his despair, there is a sense in which not only he, but all those around him, are freed to face the realities of their life together more constructively, and with fresh hope.

All of which means that for the Christian community, one of whose core images of itself is that of a body whose limbs and organs are all intimately interconnected, suicide prevention is not just a matter of providing special care for those who show signs of being most vulnerable.

From time to time, it may indeed be that. Much more profoundly, however, it is a matter of embracing in our life together the conviction that victory really does belong to the vulnerable, and that by living out this strength in weakness according to the pattern of our crucified Lord, we are both liberated and also protect one another from the worst ravages of despair.

> *For Discussion*
>
> From time to time you hear people say that they have found more truth-telling and more support in, for example, their local AA group than in their local congregation. Without becoming defensive, how might you respond to them? Or if this has been your own experience, how might you usefully explain it to others?

## 2.8　Letter from a Bereaved Mother

*A letter written by a bereaved mother, acknowledging the messages of sympathy and support sent by members of her local church on the death of her son, Mark. An exploration into the ultimate pain of a son who could not handle the confusion in his life, and who judged himself too harshly.*

Dear Friends,

I do not find this an easy letter to compose. I fear that some of you may experience what I have to say as offensive and yet to be true to myself and to Mark I feel that I must write.

Firstly I want to thank you all for your messages of sympathy and for the assurances of prayer at this dreadful time. These mean so much to us as a family. Many of you have been so kind in recent days and others have shown such love and concern for Mark down the years. With others who have been more distant I want to share something of the burden it has been to be a church leader and the mother of a gay son. So often I have felt judged, silenced or marginalised during church meetings, sermons or at the Bible-study – particularly when the subject of sexuality has arisen. Perhaps I'm over sensitive, but the feelings have been very real. I've hardly ever felt safe to reveal the depth of the mixed painful emotions that I experience.

I've been so angry when I've overheard demeaning jokes and dismissive remarks about people whose sexual orientation is different. Or when I've heard rash condemnations that pillory gay people as though they were a different species.

Most of you know how much Mark contributed to Church life, to the Youth Club, to the Young Adults' Fellowship, and to the BB, until he left home. He was my youngest child and the one about who I worried least. He was so kind and he took his commitment to Christ so seriously. I often yearned that my other sons would do likewise.

The first time he preached was a wonderful experience for us. And so many of you said how much you had been helped and comforted by his preaching over the years. People kept saying that he seemed to have an amazing understanding of pain for one so young.

I remember the evening he told us so well. We were still in shock after he had broken off his engagement to June ... we couldn't understand it; she was lovely, so suitable, and even one of our own. He came into the room; he looked frozen. 'I've something to tell you both' ... and at that moment I suddenly knew. Lots of little things I'd wondered about came together. He cried and cried as he told us and as we held him and told him how much we loved him. He knew what I was thinking: no marriage or children. What will his brothers say, and the rest of the family, and the church? I remember then what he said next 'Mam, no one in their right mind would choose to be gay with all the hatred out there. I've prayed and prayed that God would make me straight, but he hasn't. I am who I am, and I'm trying to come to terms with it and to love myself'

I didn't want him to 'come out ' particularly in Christian circles; believers can be so hard sometimes; I have been so myself. I still remember the looks, the silences, the whispers that stopped when I approached; the minister who challenged him so brusquely about his 'condition'; the people at synods or committees who just withdrew from him. And the minister who suggested that he withdraw from his church responsibilities until he had 'sorted himself out'. My idealistic son felt that God would give him the strength to weather the storm. I was more doubting.

But of course there were the kindnesses too. Those who came and revealed the secret hurts of their hearts. Those who came and just listened or who really tried to understand. Those who just accepted as though it was the most natural thing in the world. There was old Miss Willoughby, who had been his Sunday School teacher. She called me to what turned out to be her death bed. I didn't think she'd have a clue what 'gay' meant. But she did – exactly. She reminded me again and again how much God loved Mark; no matter what he is or what he does. I remember Mr McBain, who everyone thought was half cracked. He came one Easter when Mark was home to take our communion service. As he gave the invitation and Mark was hesitating in our seat, he said softly, but very clearly 'Come on lad; take it, its for sinners like us'.

Of course he left Ireland, he said it was just too difficult here. I so resent that; I feel my son was robbed from me.

You know the rest. How he still felt called to preach and eventually candidated for the ministry abroad where things are different – or so he thought. And he was turned down again, and so cruelly this time. And it was too much and he took those pills. And now my lovely son is gone.

I am so confused. My heart is torn asunder by conflicting loyalties; loyalty to my son and to so many of his friends; and loyalty to what I was always taught to be the teachings of the Bible, and the position of the church. But now I'm beginning to wonder about it all. So much has changed. You know in the Gospel Hall where I was brought up we were told that films and theatre and dancing were against the Bible's clear teaching. And of course a woman wouldn't have dreamt of praying in public. And then when I married and we joined our church, and women weren't allowed into the ministry, and no one dared to take alcohol, or be seen buying a Sunday paper. And as for gambling or the lottery ... you couldn't possibly be a true believer if you did those kinds of things. And now that's all changing. What else will change? Maybe my son suffered all that for nothing. I don't know.

Sheenagh

*Discussion and reflection*
Of all the stories gathered in this section, this one is perhaps the story that demands the most from us all. For some of us, it will be the most painful to read. For others, it will be the most difficult, or unsettling. It will make some of us very angry. Others may feel that Sheenagh's

story is one to which they simply do not know how to respond, one that is as far removed from the familiar realities of congregational life as it is possible to be.

It is important, therefore, that we allow ourselves to become aware of our initial reactions to Sheenagh's story, and of the feelings to which it gives rise in us. For having acknowledged both, it is likely that we will then be more free to consider, whether in prayer or in conversation with one another, the insights that Sheenagh's story may hold for us and for the congregations and the wider Church to which we belong.

For one of the inescapable realities to which Sheenagh's story points is that, within the Christian churches, some aspects of what we have received as uncontested scriptural teaching on human sexuality are now being questioned and re-examined in new ways. And some of those who are raising these questions and prompting this re-examination are gay and lesbian Christians and their friends and families. It is simply no longer possible, if indeed it ever was, to say that there is only one valid Christian perspective on these matters, when the difficult truth, difficult for all of us, is that mature, committed, and thoughtful Christian people can argue for a number of diverse understandings, and all on biblical grounds.

This does not mean, of course, that nothing of what we may regard as traditional Christian teaching on human sexuality has any continuing validity. It simply means that the whole area of human sexuality and its right expression is contested in a large number of Christian churches today. It is important to know what our own tradition or denomination teaches, and to give these teachings careful consideration. But no Christian Church worthy of the name should ever be in the business of attempting to stifle conversation on an issue of importance about which Christians of good faith and character disagree, and disagree profoundly.

And yet if we accept this much, we immediately face another problem. Much of Sheenagh's anger and frustration and confusion were linked to the many silences which, in her experience, were imposed on her and on those she loved. She is not able to say that the church was a place in which she could talk freely about her son, and his life, and her love for him, as she was not prepared to edit out her growing understanding of the truth of who Mark was. And when people did learn that Mark was gay, many of them resorted to silence and withdrawal, and thus continued to deny to Sheenagh the possibility of conversation, and Mark the experience of continuing acceptance.

We may therefore have to face the fact that when the churches maintain an official position that imposes an automatic silence on those whose experience and whose grasp of the truth lead them to question this official position, real conversation will be almost impossible. Or to put it more clearly, as long as there is a significant power imbalance in Church conversations on human sexuality, as long as gay and lesbian Christians and their friends cannot reveal the truth of who they are or talk openly and honestly about their own experience without running the risk of losing their jobs or being rejected by the very community in which they were baptised, then for so long is it likely to be impossible for the churches to address issues of human sexuality with any measure of depth and responsibility.

And if any denomination's teaching on human sexuality has the effect of precluding our having the very open-hearted and prayerful conversations we need to have with one another, then surely our teaching needs to be re-examined. For Sheenagh and Mark (and his brothers and sisters in every congregation in our Church), they deserve no less from us.

# SOCIAL AND HIGH-RISK FACTORS

## 3.1 Overview

Suicide is the final, destructive act that destroys one's life. It is the end result of a developed sense of complete failure. Life has no further meaning. Its common purpose is to find a solution to a perceived problem to which there seems no other answer.

> Suicide is not a disease. It is an expression of a host of emotions, hopelessness, guilt, sorrow, loneliness, rage, fear and shame that have their roots in psychological, social, medical and biochemical factors
>
> *(Psychological Society of Ireland, 1992)*

Suicide has been described as:
* the final tantrum
* an understandable reaction or response to complete isolation, neglect or social disruption

- the last episode of hopelessness and humiliation
- the last tragedy
- the unforgivable sin
- mad, bad, or irresponsible
- the end closure of a story-line

All such descriptions are negative in word and tone; they are final in epitomising hopelessness and helplessness.

Statistics indicate some changes that show a significant alteration in the pattern of those who are at risk of suicide – whether attempted or successful. The rates of male/female suicides show a change from 2.5:1 to about 4.5:1. The increase in suicide rates for the elderly, those living alone, farmers, young men and some who work in stressful situations in the professions are also significant.

In 1994, the under-25 year age group in Northern Ireland accounted for 27 per cent of suicide deaths, the vast majority being male. There is a peak in the 18–25 year age group. In 1997, in Republic of Ireland, 111 young people ended their lives, 95 of which were male. Young men are not so adept at forming small peer support groups where they can be open about inner turmoil and self-doubt. 'Lad' culture demands they drink and play hard but never divulge inner hurts or personal pain for fear of showing weakness. This pattern continues into adult and elderly life. For one hundred and twenty-three years, until 1993, suicide was a criminal act in the Republic of Ireland (in Northern Ireland the law was changed in 1961), adding to the pain and distress of family and friends as they struggle to come to terms with their loss

*Chosen methods* for suicide have, over time, shown a clearly identifiable pattern and distinction between males and females.

- Males: hanging, gun-shot injury, jumping off bridges and cliff-tops
- Females: drug overdose
- Both groups may use drowning

There are many myths, that:

- those who talk about it, do not try – *Not True*
- a good job and a stable home provide safety from suicide – *Not True*
- those who try and fail will not try again – *Not True*
- those who attempt suicide really want to die – *Not Necessarily True*

There are three distinguishing types of suicide:

- completed suicide, described as death by suicide
- failed suicide. An attempted act, designed to end life, which fails because of insufficient effort on the part of the victim or due to intervention by another person or persons and with the help of subsequent medical procedures.
- para-suicide. This is a self-destructive type act, which may be described as an impulsive act or as 'a cry for help'. Para-suicide does not succeed.

It now becomes necessary to consider and describe the risk factors, vulnerability, indications of suicidal intent, signs, symptoms and feelings that combine to lead to an action, final in its concept, which is intended to be the end response to single or multiple factors such as isolation, neglect, conflict, social disruption or the end-story of a severe psychological disturbance. Some of these factors may be considered to overlap, leading to what have been described as the Commonalities of Suicide.

*Commonalities of Suicide* (Schnncidman 1990)
1. The common purpose is to seek a solution.
2. The common goal is to achieve a permanent cessation of consciousness.
3. The common stimulus is intolerable psychological pain.
4. The common emotion is hopelessness / helplessness.
5. The common stress factors are frustrated psychological needs.

## 3.2 Factors Leading to or Causing Suicide

*Whether complete, failed or the situation described as para-suicide.*

*Risk factors* may be demonstrated –

- in those who are vulnerable because of inherent developmental, psychiatric or personality inadequacies. In this group persons may be unable to achieve a degree of maturity, a career structure or satisfying personal relationships. Such persons may not have the strength of mind, character or the necessary support group to protect them. Society has been slow to understand the needs of these people and in many situations their needs are not met, leading to the danger that one or more of the commonalities described above may lead to a final tragedy
- in those who become vulnerable due to exposure to crises, disappointments and/or psychiatric illness

The following risk factors may apply to both groups described above:

- Poverty, making it difficult/impossible to create a meaningful life-style for self or family members
- Emotional, physical or sexual abuse, including rape, in childhood, adolescence or in adult life
- Isolation, especially in the elderly, those living alone, without neighbours or family support
- Multiple loss and family break-down
- Faulty emotional attachment patterns
- Chronically-impaired self-esteem
- Membership of deprived or marginalised groups in society
- Chronic unemployment
- Acute/chronic substance abuse
- Chronic life-threatening illness

- Alienation from family or peer group
- Lack of a life-meaning support system
- A victim of bullying
- Many psychiatric illnesses may lead to pain and feelings that life is not worth-while and that death would be a release

Signs of suicidal intent are factors described by family, friends or by professional support persons:

- Loss of interest and concentration
- Withdrawal of social contact
- Personal neglect
- Talking about ending life
- History of suicide in the family
- Earlier attempts at suicide are particularly significant
- Painful or disabling illness
- A recent bereavement or the break-up of a close relationship
- Drug dependency
- Current unhappy changes in health or other circumstances, e.g. retirement and/or financial problems
- Depression may be severe, sub-clinical or may go unrecognised for the serious clinical condition that it is

Symptoms are described by the person at risk, who may identify some of the risk factors listed above.

Persons in crisis or illness frequently lose insight and understanding into their situation, particularly an understanding of emotional psychological, psychiatric and spiritual needs. These may be expressed in terms such as:

- an inability to relate to others
- feelings of being alone, even in the presence of others
- feeling that he/she cannot measure up to family or friends in ability or success
- constantly dwelling on problems, with no answers.

- loss of energy, either mental or physical
- unable to keep his/her mind on issues for any length of time
- a loss of emotion, unable to feel emotion, whether loving, joy, hating or anger
- alteration to sleep/eating patterns
- may express not having any interest in living – and may express thoughts of wanting to die

People often show their suicidal feelings by:

- being withdrawn and unable to relate to others (quiet, sit in a corner away from others).
- having definite ideas about how to attempt suicide, maybe speaking of tidying up personal affairs or giving indications that suicide is being planned.
- talking about feeling terribly alone
- expressing feelings of uselessness and failure; of hopelessness and a total lack of a sense of being a real person
- constantly dwelling on problems for which there seem to be no answers.
- Expressing the lack of any supporting philosophy of life – 'life has no meaning'
- Many will express feelings of a real loss of a spiritual life and describe having lost any sense of the presence of God

*Feelings* may be described as; desolation, confusion, sadness, guilt, anger, hopelessness, helplessness, loneliness, isolation and phrases like:

> *'The only choice'*
> *'I do not want to live'*
> *'I want to die'*
> *'I cannot find any meaning'*

## 3.3 Factors Leading to Suicidal Intent May be Divided into Several Classes

Having listed and summarised the risks, signs, symptoms and feelings, it is imperative to look in depth at certain factors in suicide intent that contribute to suicide attempts, whether complete, failed, or para-suicide.

It is accepted that in over 90 per cent of complete or failed suicide, there are common factors of a sense of hopelessness and a measure of depression.

Hopelessness and helplessness do not develop instantly, they are the result of long-term life factors that did not or could not be removed or alleviated. A sense of hopelessness can develop from many different factors, either single, or more often, multiple. It may begin in childhood, with painful experiences or a sense of rejection by parents, siblings or other family members. A lack of attainment in social situations or in school, often associated with a feeling of unpopularity or which may result from being bullied – or may result in bullying behaviour that is often brought on by a sense of failure.

If such factors are not dealt with – or are inadequately dealt with – the resulting lack of confidence can have an effect on career opportunities, creating meaningful relationships and family life. The later stages of continuing failure, or of a perception of failure, may lead to feelings of sadness or to a sense of helplessness. When there are no positive factors to counteract negative feelings or experiences, a sense of hopelessness and even depression may ensue and finally the development of feelings that life is not worth living.

These may be summarised as:

*Experiential*
Emotional, physical or sexual abuse in childhood or adolescence. This may result from lack of bonding with parents, by belonging to a dysfunctional family, with

habits of violence or living with siblings, carers or other adults who do not offer love or who simply do not care.

## Social
There are many factors in social relationships, in school, neighbourhood, student, or leisure relationships that can cause pain or feelings of failure. These can include drift into drug addiction, choosing 'bad' company, with those whose values are harmful, loose sexual relationships where habits develop of having frequently different sexual partners with no security in a relationship that is seen as solely for sexual gratification. Jealousy and envy in social, student or work situations may lead to feelings of failure, especially when associated with a lack of confidence.

## Alteration in social relationships
These may be real or perceived when compared with others.
- Social and economic isolation
- Family break-down
- Faulty attachment patterns
- Membership of a deprived or marginalised group.
- Failure in study or work programmes may lead to loss of friendships or a feeling of inequality in comparison with others.

## Emotional
In childhood this may be due to lack of parental love or sense of security. It may result from a lack of close relationships with parents, siblings or other family members. If a loss or bereavement is not adequately dealt with, a sense of continuing sadness may become a real depression. Chronically impaired self-esteem is often apparent in those who have not chosen a career that well suits their gifts or who have experienced failure in social or learning environments.

An irrational and continual preoccupation with guilt is frequently a component of suicidal intent. The loss or erosion of trust in others leads to a sense of isolation and fear.

## Failure

Can be defined as a lack of meaning in life. May be the result of chronic unemployment, and/or a lack of career success.

This sense of failure may lead to an increasing preoccupation with removing issues that are a cause for concern and anxiety.

## Sexuality

Issues around sexuality can arise in many ways. If people are confused or troubled in their gender identity and/or sexual maturity, and lack support, or if they are marginalised and/or rejected because of their identity, the resulting anxiety and stress can be a factor leading to suicidal intent.

*Heterosexual relations* – there are men and women who may have difficulties and a lack of confidence in developing a deep relationship and such difficulties may lead to deep unhappiness and distress.

*Confused gender identity* – this is the term used to describe those who cannot come to terms with their sexual identity.

*Homosexual persons and relationships* – Gays (men) and lesbians (women) – this attraction may lead to a relationship or may be recognised by feelings that are controlled and may lead to great loneliness and introspection.

*Homophobia* – homophobia may often lead to a sense of rejection and isolation on the part of those attracted to same sex relationships and cause deep confusion and depression. Such intolerance may force gays (more frequently) and lesbians (rarely) to feel that they cannot continue to live and that suicide may be the only solution. The rates of attempted or completed suicide are not high but for any one person to feel so much intolerance and rejection as to make life not worth while is one too many.

Similarly, *Bisexuals*, *Transvestites* and *Transsexuals* often keep their needs and behaviour secret through fear of shame or rejection

*Depression*
Many psychiatric illnesses may lead to suicidal intent; perhaps one that can most easily be understood is clinical depression. A number of researchers and workers in this field have said that in all suicides there is at least an element of depression.

Depression may be:
- A genuine reaction to a situation of loss or other problem. Bereavement is a process that is very personal to each bereaved person and each needs to respond in his/her own way and time.
- A severe clinical condition with well-developed suicidal intent. Signs and symptoms would be present in a severe form of those listed earlier in this chapter.

Many people suffering from depression have strong feelings of guilt and shame and feel they should be able to change a depressive mood by will-power; these feelings may be reinforced by family and friends. The reality is much less easy and professional help is needed to make a diagnosis and treat the process of depression; support groups need to understand and accept that mood swings cannot be controlled at will or with chosen words of advice.

Understanding professionals and counsellors can begin the healing process by first believing that the situation is real and second by being prepared to listen. The resulting discussion needs to recognise that feelings and resulting behaviour can be helped. Medical intervention may also include carefully chosen medication which, to be effective, must be taken regularly, as ordered – and this will take time.

It can be a real relief to have feelings brought into the open, acknowledged, believed and discussed and positive ways of coping offered to the sufferer. A person with a serious clinical depression may not be able to express a reason for his/her feelings – he/she is just depressed with associated symptoms. Physically obvious signs are sleep/eating disturbance, a loss of concentration and interest; tiredness and weariness of mind and body are very real and there are often feelings of utter loneliness and desolation that cannot be described. There may be a real loss of insight into personal feelings and behaviour. Persons may become hypersensitive to failure and rejection, which may be real or perceived, and look for approval and praise that may not be accepted. Guilt feelings may be very real and associated with a sense of the loss of spiritual life, if this had been a reality before the depression developed, and if not understood this may exacerbate feelings of guilt and unworthiness.

Suicidal ideas may be very real and it would be helpful and important to identify reasons to live. Every person is unique and valued; the love and friendship of family, friends and neighbours is an integral part of being a complete person. For those who would have had a belief in God and for whom a spiritual life is important it may help to accept that life is not owned by each person. If it is not accepted that life came from God, then at least we can understand that it was given by parents. We are all a part of the human race and unique in our identity.

Suicide is the last, final tragic action; it cannot put us beyond God's infinite love (one writer, describing his own experience of depression asks 'Are suicide victims especially loved by God because of the agony?')

## 3.4    Intervention

It would be important that every person suffering from even mild reactive depression (and certainly if there is evidence of severe depression as demonstrated by signs and symptoms), when life has become apparently worthless and negative, should be advised to visit his/her General Practitioner. Pastoral care should be offered by those who have experience in the field.

An *emergency* is a situation requiring immediate intervention.

1. Common examples are: passive neglect, self-inflicted injury, attempted suicide, completed suicide, distressed family and friends.
2. It can occur in any location: home, work-place, city street, open country.
3. Emergency action includes: care of suicidal person, care of those in a supporting role, family, friends, neighbours; call for medical and pastoral help.
4. Prevention: prevent self injury and violence to others
5. Do not leave them alone if actively suicidal.

*What to do*
- Engage the person in the emergency situation in meaningful conversation and listen carefully, without interruption to what he or she has to say
- Create a safe place
- Get help as needed
- Care also for supporters and family

*Who to go to*
- Family, Friends, colleagues
- Medical help
- Pastoral support
- Samaritans

*How far to act*
- Advise
- Counselling and pastoral care – connect with professionals
- Support family and friends as appropriate

FROM DESPAIR TO HOPE

## 3.5   Conclusion

In the hopelessness and meaningless feelings of depression, when the only answer seems to be an act of final tragedy, when the guiding beacon of God's light has become dark, it is possible to find the nearness of God 'inside' and to discover that the search for meaning, the search for oneself and the search for God are finally all the same thing.

It is in the depths that 'our lives are hid with Christ in God'

In that seeking inwards to the centre of being and life, it is our understanding that we are all God's children, deserving of acceptance and dignity in all areas of life, no matter what circumstances life puts us in; even in complete desolation and helplessness, God will lift us up.

# PART II

# RESPONDING AS INDIVIDUALS

*This second section builds on the first section, exploring some aspects of a pastoral response, primarily from the perspective of the individual – minister, priest, church leader, youth worker, friend, and so on.*

# THEOLOGICAL
# REFLECTION

## 4.1 Spreading a Table in the Wilderness

There is something irreducibly particular about each story we tell or hear of suicide or attempted suicide. And there is a sense in which our reflections on the particular stories, outlined in chapter two, of Mary, Billy, Jacob, Michael, Eithne, Liam, and Sheenagh, can only acknowledge and respect the specific anguish and precisely unrepeatable circumstances of their lives, into which we can never fully enter and which led, for them, to a place of attempted or completed suicide.

This reverence, if that is not too hard a word to use in these circumstances, before the particular and often incomprehensible pain of one person's story, is required not least of the Christian community, which affirms the named and recognisable and irreplaceable identity and value of each human person. And it may seem, therefore, that the particular forms of heartbreak experienced by Mary, Billy, Jacob, Michael, Eithne, Liam, and Sheenagh should not be combed over by us for traces of insight, or for reassurance that we and those we love would never finally make the choices to which they felt irrevocably drawn.

And yet precisely because each human life is particular and unrepeatable, all Christian theological reflection has to take place amidst the messiness and uncertainties of human living. We wrestle with the meaning of the biblical witness in particular, urgent circumstances of our own, just as the human authors of the biblical texts struggled with their own pre-occupations, changing contexts, and constant interruptions. In the Acts of the Apostles, for example, events as simple as a disturbing vision at night, a gathering of women at the river, sudden shouting at an open window, a shipwreck off the coast of Malta, and the raucous singing of hymns at night, as well as the sudden appearance of death, all invite and require from the community of believers a fresh and urgent reflection on the lively presence of the Spirit.

And as we have seen, for those of us who belong to the Christian churches today, it is still often those experiences that are most painful, most disturbing, and most difficult to comprehend that are able to provide us with the most fruitful soil for ongoing theological reflection. And that is why the decision to engage in this process is indeed to honour the very particular lives, with their public, told stories and their hidden, wordless silences, who in their living and in their dying have been part of our own. And so it is to this process of ongoing reflection that we now turn.

In our respectful hearing of the stories of Mary, Jacob, Billy, Michael, Liam, Sheenagh, and Eithne, we have been observing the distinction between a fruitless attempt to rewrite the past ('If only she had done this ... or he had said that ...'), and a willingness to imagine, through these narratives, the possibility of new story lines both for ourselves and for others.

And so we have wrestled together with hard and difficult insights: the ways in which the familiar structures of our families and communities can become idolatrous, simply through our failure to look critically at their effects; the situations in which our evangelical courage has failed us, and in our congregations we have preferred the safety of the known to the freedom of the unknown; the extent to which the churches must work out in a fresh way, for each new generation and context, the shape of their public witness to the gospel; the many ways in which we are tempted to close and protect our lives, rather than opening them to the surprising vulnerability of a life lived under the grace of God; the ordinary, unremarkable, and daily ways in which we fail one another, but also in which we sustain one another, in our complex and often fragmented lives; the painful necessity of having to find ways to attend, in responsible and respectful conversations, to the very real differences among us; and the extent to which even familiar and basic Christian concepts like that of sin may sometimes need to be articulated and understood in new ways.

But now, having honoured these stories for the insights which, in their telling, they have enabled among us, we are ready to turn over yet another layer of ground, and in sifting through its rich darkness together, rediscover some of the deepest roots of our Christian faith.

## 4.2    Choosing Life Among the Shadows

One of the assumptions upon which most people base their lives, whether consciously or not, is that life is on the whole worth living, or at the very least, that in the matter of living, we have little choice. What one does with a life is to live it out, whether with a sense of adventure or a sense of just dealing with one day at a time. 'Life goes on', we say to each other, as if it were impossible for things to be otherwise.

And so when an older man, like Michael, or an 18 year old, like Billy, decides to take his own life, decides, in fact, that 'getting on with life' is either impossible or less preferable than the alternative, one of our core assumptions is challenged at its very heart. Michael's wife put it very well when she said that her husband's suicide had broken a taboo, and the broken taboo was to voice the possibility, in words or in actions, that sometimes death is indeed preferable to life.

And the breaking of this taboo is as uncomfortable for Christians as for anyone else. Our faith teaches us that human life is a gift from God, renewed in love at every moment of our living and breathing and dreaming. To refuse such a gift, or to tire of its demands and seek to return it, seems both ungrateful and defiant in ways that frighten and disturb us. And what is perhaps even more terrifying is the thought that if life can be dealt with simply by ending it, then the whole created order, with its rhythms of tides and harvests, setting sun and rising moon, wind and calm waters, birth and childhood and maturity, is thrown off balance, and life, for those of us who continue to live it, becomes fundamentally precarious and unreliable.

And yet perhaps we need to listen again to some of the stories we have just heard, and to the biblical story. Few choices, in the minds of those who make them, appear as stark as the choice between life and death. Our lives and our dilemmas are often more shadowed and tangled in character than they are clear and unambiguous, and this is no less true for those who take their own lives than it is for everyone else. Michael's decision to end his life was a decision to die. And yet, to continue his life in the way that he had always known it was no longer a choice that he had. And thus it may have seemed to him that the only choices available to him were two kinds of dying.

Billy, too, was in his own way confronted with this same choice. His letter reveals a young man thirsting for life, in the form of a father he could trust, an education founded on respect for the young and enjoyment of their energy, a community to which to belong. And yet he came to feel that life was not something he could choose, but something that was being taken from him, and in that situation, dying before he had lost everything seemed better than the alternative.

Now it is very important to notice that the point here is not to 'explain' why either of these men took his own life. In the end, there are no explanations, and the darkness in which either man decided to do what he did will always remain shrouded in mystery, known only to himself and to God. The point is rather to acknowledge that human life rarely if ever presents us with a series of clear and unambiguous decisions, in which choosing life and choosing death are polar opposites. Rather, we each experience a lifetime of choices, both conscious and hidden, which are streaked with light and shadow, clarity and darkness, inertia and hope, and it is the midst of this changing light, and only here, that we live.

But this makes the broken taboo even more terrifying. Not only did Michael appear to believe that death had become preferable to life, he also, in his dying, revealed the complexity and pain and fragility of his life, and of the lives of those around him who from now on, and until their own deaths, would in some way be coping with his.

And though we might wish it otherwise, our Christian faith does not exempt us in any way from this complexity and ambiguity. It does, however, offer us at its heart another story, a story that gives us few answers, but that does give us a fresh and perhaps even compelling perspective on these complex and sometimes painful and often difficult human lives of ours.

And the story, of course, is that of the incarnation. It is the story of God's choosing of life, of God's unequivocal choosing of the living out of a human life, in all its complexity and sorrow and ambiguity, until its very not-chosen ending. And the importance of God's unequivocal choosing of human life in this way is found not in judgement but in embrace. In other words, God's choosing, far from being a judgement on those who have been unable to make the same choice, is in fact an expression of solidarity with them in their pain, their confusion, their absent choices. And for us, who live, God's choosing is also an act of embrace, and an affirmation that God knows and understands what it is to have to assent, again and again, to a human life that itself embraces not only the possibility but also the reality of failure and death, as well as that of gratitude and joy.

We still live in this changing light, negotiating our lives between clarity and darkness. But we do so knowing that the God in whom we put our trust has unequivocally chosen life with us among these shadows, this light. And knowing, too, that it is this story of God's choosing, and not the narrative of our own broken choices, which will give to our lives their final shape and beauty.

### 4.3 Being Christian, Being Human

One of the convictions of the Christian believer is that it is in Christ that we become most truly ourselves, most truly human, our faces bearing most clearly the image that God created us to bear. Or to put it another way, it is Jesus Christ who, in his humanity, shows us how to live in perfect freedom and trust before God, and thus offers us a pattern for the life we share as the body of Christ.

In this understanding, therefore, there is no contradiction between being human, and being Christian. And yet it is often hard not to draw the conclusion that many Christians, no less than others and often much more than some, are ill at ease with their own humanity. And nowhere does this become more pronounced than in the whole area of pain and suffering.

Of course human lives are made up of much more than suffering and pain. At the same time, however, there is no human life, fully lived, that has not known them both, and that has not become acquainted with their accompanying heartbreak. In this sense, suffering and pain are two of the authentic marks of a life that is human, though of course there are others. And yet all too frequently one encounters both congregations and individual Christians who have arranged their lives in such a way as to attempt not only to exclude pain and suffering, but also to distance themselves from the deeply disturbing feelings that can follow unannounced in the wake of any experience of profound anguish or grief, particularly when it seems as if one's life is simply coming apart at the seams.

And so it is that in some Christian congregations a wedge is driven between the experience of being human and the experience of being Christian. This rarely happens deliberately, of course, or with any conscious destructive intent. It is much more likely to come about as a result of the longing, which we probably all share, that our Christian lives will speak more clearly of hope than of despair, more persuasively of joy than of grief.

And yet if this longing is applied prescriptively to the lives of individual believers and particular congregations, it can result in the opposite of what was no doubt intended, that is, Christians who have lost their credibility because they appear to have lost their humanity, who preach not redemption but human vulnerability as failure. And what is worse, by pushing suffering to the margins of the Christian life, they become incapable of bearing witness to the core biblical insight that God is present in suffering. And thus God, too, is pushed to the margins.

Our theological reflections on suicide therefore require us to reflect on how, as Christians, we live our humanity before others. And this reflection has at least three dimensions.

First, it prompts us to recognise that our fragility and vulnerability as human beings are not flaws in our humanity, but two of its defining features. Of course this is not to deny the ways in which any of us can and do also show courage and resilience. But it is to make a very important, and for us in Western Europe, a very counter-cultural affirmation. In the language of the biblical tradition, humanity is shaped by God from the dust of the ground, and enlivened by God's own breath, and in the mercy and kindness of God, that breath of life in us is renewed at every moment. Therefore our fragility is not an unfortunate side effect of our creation, and still less is it a consequence of sin or of a ruptured relationship with God. It is rather nothing less than an inherent feature of the created goodness of our humanity.

And so in the face of the ever-present temptation to value persons on the basis of their achievements, coping skills, and competence, there is perhaps an urgent need to reflect further on the gentleness of God towards us, precisely on the basis of our created fragility. To be unable to act independently or to 'make it' without reference to those around us is not an indictment, as Liam, for example, perhaps came to feel that it was. Still less is it a cause for shame. It is rather a core feature of our created humanity, one to be celebrated by believers, and incorporated without embarrassment into our understanding of ourselves.

Second, however, our humanity is lived not only in recognition of our own created fragility, but also in constant awareness of the generosity of God towards us, and to which the most appropriate response is praise. Praise and thanksgiving are at the core of the Christian life, and yet they are often trivialised and misunderstood. If we see them as being incompatible with grief or suffering, or indeed, in their expression, as a denial of grief and suffering, then they can easily become one more example of the dangerous uncoupling of being human and being Christian.

What could it have meant, we might ask, for Jacob to have praised God in the face of the closure of his congregation and the disappearance of his community of faith? If the language of praise seems awkward or inappropriate to us in this context, then perhaps we need to think again about what we mean by praise and thanksgiving. Whatever else the act of praise may entail, it must certainly not entail a denial of everything that can tempt a person or a community to despair. When our understanding of 'praise' is narrowed down to refer only to a particular style of music for worship whose lyrics express only a certain range of emotions, this danger of denial is very real.

And yet the apostle Paul teaches that we are to give thanks in all circumstances. Somehow, therefore, we must come to an understanding of praise that is able to embrace all of human life, its sorrows and its grief as well as its hope and its joy. Such an understanding of praise and thanksgiving will not be naive, or deny in its expression the realities of pain. It will rather be understood as an affirmation of God's generosity towards us, often in ways we can scarcely grasp or imagine, and as an act of empowerment in the face of circumstances that may yet tempt us to despair. And the empowerment comes not from any expectation that God will shield us from the depths of our own humanity, depths from which even God has chosen not to be shielded. The empowerment comes rather from an awareness of the trustworthiness of God towards us precisely in our humanity and vulnerability, for it is in this same fragile humanity that God created us and is bringing us, even now, to new life.

Third and finally, if we are able to praise God in this way, both for our created humanity and for God's generosity and faithfulness to us precisely as fragile human beings, then we are also free to acknowledge that the very human experiences of hopelessness, grief, betrayal and anger are not alien to people who inhabit the biblical tradition. In fact, the truth is quite the reverse. What is alien to the biblical tradition is to deny the devastating power of such experiences, or to try to convince ourselves that believers are in some way protected from their impact.

Mary, for example, suffered from feelings of depression and hopelessness and from a sense of abandonment and isolation within her own family. And it is tempting, when we witness such feelings in others, to minimise them, or when we experience them ourselves, to deny their power. And yet we need to acknowledge how deeply these feelings and experiences are rooted in the biblical tradition. Even the sense of having been abandoned by God is in no way alien to the narrative of our faith, a truth to which the Psalms most clearly and repeatedly attest.

And thus in living out both our humanity and our Christian identity before others, we must take care never to abandon this truth: that while the last word of God to us is always one of hope and life and freedom, God refuses, at the same time, to stifle the voices of our anguish and pain. Those voices, whether they belong to us or to others, are truth-telling voices. They do not tell the whole truth, but if we deny them or do not permit them to come to church, then we are in some way rejecting God's own passionate choice for us, that we might live our created lives to the full, in all their vulnerability and all their abundance.

## 4.4    Forgiveness And The Failure of Imagination

Among the most profound and troubling questions that encounters with suicide are likely to raise for the Christian churches is that of forgiveness, what it means and how it functions in devastated and broken lives. And here the urgency of our need for understanding arises largely from the fact that while there are some acts of destruction and some experiences of loss for which a significant degree of restitution can be made, suicide is not one of them. In its most significant effects, suicide is both irreversible and final.

And thus the question of forgiveness arises in a number of guises, each one more poignant than the next. For some surviving family members and friends, the only question worth asking is how to forgive someone they loved for taking her own life, and indeed, in some cases, whether or not they can or should do so. For others, the focus of forgiveness, or of the seeming impossibility of forgiveness, is the self. In other words, how can I ever forgive myself for not seeing, not helping, and not preventing him from doing this terrible thing?

And even if one can work out what the practice of forgiveness might mean in either of these contexts, terrible and painful gaps remain. The slow learning of forgiveness does not, whatever else it might do, make suicide understandable. It does not provide explanations. Still less does it protect us from the ongoing and disturbing realisation that our lives can be interrupted at any time by events both incomprehensible and previously unimaginable to us. And neither does the practice of forgiveness necessarily eliminate the effects of suicide upon the bereaved, whether those effects be focused by a sense of wounded betrayal or by a debilitating awareness of one's own limitations and powerlessness as a human being.

And then, of course, there are the struggles with forgiveness undertaken by those who decide to end their own lives. Eithne had become convinced that her only hope for a different life lay with her father, and that if she were ever to have any kind of a future, her father would need to begin to give that future shape by admitting to the extent of his wrongdoing. It was, therefore, impossible for Eithne even to begin to reflect on whether the practice of forgiveness might offer to her another way forward, or on what such a practice might look like in her situation. And what relevance could the practice of forgiveness have had for Sheenagh's son, Mark, when the attitudes and policies of his Church continued both to deny, on a daily basis, his experience and his insight, and to justify that denial?

And so perhaps the first and most important thing that needs to be said is that the precise shape and form that the practice of forgiveness may take in any of the circumstances we have been considering cannot be delineated or fixed in advance. The hard work involved in discerning how forgiveness might be practised and embodied in any given context is both a necessary discipline and an inescapable one. And yet in reflecting on the experience of suicide in the Christian community, there are at least two core assumptions that will help to ground a way forward through this process of discernment.

The first, which always bears repeating, is that forgiveness, at least as it is understood in the biblical tradition, is not about trying to forget the past, or to deny that it ever happened, or to minimise its effects. Those who find themselves attempting to do any of those things are not seeking to practice forgiveness. On the contrary, they are attempting to do away with the need to do so. They are seeking a wholly understandable relief from pain that we have probably all undertaken in one way or another. But relief from pain is not the same thing as the practice of forgiveness.

The second, and more important assumption, however, is that a starting point for the practice of forgiveness is to understand it as a process of uncoupling or untying the present from the past, and the future from the present. It remains true that we are indelibly marked by many of the things that we have experienced, that we have done, or that have been done to us. And yet the starting point for the practice of forgiveness is the affirmation that our lives as they are lived in the present, our choices, our attitudes, and our character, are not finally hostage to the past. They are shaped, finally and most profoundly, not by the scars we bear but by the mercy and generosity and love of God.

And so, too, with the future. When the present is wholly coloured by the experience of debilitating grief and

FROM DESPAIR TO HOPE

inertia, and is perhaps also, as in Mark's case, warped by the experience of continuing marginalisation, not only can it seem that the present has become unliveable, but also that the possibility of a future is being daily destroyed. And it is precisely here, when the practice of forgiveness seems most impossible, and the very concept of forgiveness itself most devoid of meaning, that the image of the future being untied from the present becomes most powerful. For to affirm that such an uncoupling is possible, against what often seems like all the evidence, is to reaffirm our trust in a God whose very character is defined by the creation out of nothing of something new, by the creation out of death of the possibility of something green and fresh and tender and alive.

In some respects, our struggles with the practice of forgiveness, in whatever context, represent simply a failure of imagination on our part, an incapacity to imagine that things could ever possibly be different. And so it is at precisely these times of struggle that our greatest hope lies in remembering this: that God suffers from no such failure, and that the future that is being prepared for us is both greater and more trustworthy than we can yet imagine.

# PASTORAL ISSUES AND REFLECTIONS

In March 2000 Sydney Callaghan prepared a first draft of what was to be his contribution to this study and information booklet on suicide. At that time the initial signs of his own mortality were already becoming evident. He died in February 2001 without having been able to develop further his content plan. Sydney was a Methodist minister of rare commitment. Central to his understanding of the Christian life was his belief that 'people, only people, matter'. Expounding the Sermon on the Mount he disclosed a faith formula of sublime simplicity – people first, principles second, property last. In his ministry he travelled in the capital cities of Belfast and Dublin and across Ireland as Convenor for Evangelism of the Methodist Church. A co-founder of the Belfast Samaritans, Sydney gave his all to the lonely, the sick at heart, the disturbed of mind, the dispossessed, the marginalised. Available to those who needed help at any hour of the day or night, there was no other person better equipped to disclose, from the personal experience of ministry, the pastoral insights and theological wisdom that should illuminate our understanding of the reality of suicide. I have undertaken to elaborate his notes as faithfully as I can as a tribute to our friendship over forty years and to his role as teacher and mentor in my own life. – *Salters Sterling*

## 5.1 Setting the Context

Sydney began his draft with the statement – 'The term suicide sounds so sinister, like death, another taboo word that people shy away from and don't want to talk about.' That is profoundly true. Death in all its forms has the effect of sending a tremor through all our existences. St Paul, writing to the Church in Corinth about Christ risen from the dead and become the first-fruits of those that slept, continues, 'For he must reign till he has put all enemies under his feet. The last enemy that shall be destroyed is death.' Put like that, nothing could be more incisively clear. Life experience teaches us to accept some death as part of the order of things. A very old person can fade away with very little, if any, of the trauma of dying. On the other hand the death of a child, the death of a teenager, the death of a parent with a young family, the death of a recently retired friend, the death of a sibling; these deaths vibrate the foundations of our own life. And it is ever so. In comparison, the effect of suicide is much further up the Richter scale that measures the foundation-shaking events of life. It makes evident how tenuous can be our hold on living. It reveals how fragile can be the ground of our being. It signals how disturbingly ephemeral can be the nature of our personhood. In an instant and for a very long moment that can seem like all eternity, the value system of living and loving is stood on its head. Our breath is caught and it is not that words fail, it is rather that there are no words.

Sydney continues: 'the reality is that death is a universal experience and sadly suicide a phenomenon on the increase in this country.' We have become painfully aware of how prevalent suicide is among young men between the ages of 15 years and 24 years and among a wider age group in the rural community. But suicide is not a respecter of age or gender or class or creed or condition. Some of those closest to me who have died through suicide have been in the ministry of the Church and most certainly not just one denomination. Others have been in the first flush of youth, all-rounders in sport and in academe, on the threshold of all the world counts success. Only a few have given evidence of the kind of disturbance of mind or spirit that we all want to think of as essentially inherent in those who take their own lives. We will be defeated if we set out to find common elements of a universal profile.

In the less than six months since I was invited to contribute this piece three of my friends and acquaintances have attempted suicide. None of them conform to the perceived profile of such people. Two died. One did not. Two were women. One was a man. Two were in their 40s or thereabouts. One was over seventy. To the observer all had some reasonable reason for doing what they did. One had a diagnosis of terminal illness to be endured in the context of a broken marriage. One was burdened with constant suffering, the pain of which was beyond relief and whose life partner of more than fifty years had just died. One could see no shape to the future. None of them had a diagnosis of mental ill-health. Together and separately they raise just the kind of issues that need to be addressed when considering the pastoral responsibilities of the people of God.

Before attempting to investigate those issues further let me try to construct a theological perspective that will help to elucidate both the questions and the answers.

## 5.2    Theological Reflections

The Christian faith functions within a framework, the beginning and end of which is a vision of life without death.

In the beginning, in Genesis, death as a feature of human experience does not enter into the picture. In the end, in Revelation, peace and healing are constantly created and re-created and life is forever and forever a reality. In between death with birth is the universal constant. It is the last great enemy. And in between stands Jesus. It is in the acceptance of responsibility for his own death, as much as for his own life, that the ministry of Jesus is transformed from the ordinary into the extraordinary. Calvary discloses the mortal – 'My God, My God, why hast thou forsaken me?' and the immortal, the triumphant, 'It is accomplished'. That shout of triumph illuminates the key features of the life and work of Jesus for all time and for all eternity. He went about doing good and healing all manner of diseases. The essential ingredient in all his teaching and all his doing was concerned with social and personal health and wholeness, physical, moral, psychological, spiritual, for individuals, for groups, for nations, for human kind, and for all creation, in time and in eternity.

Within a generation of his going to the Father the groups of those who remained faithful and those who became faithful were described in many different ways – the household of God, the congregation of the faithful, a royal priesthood, a holy nation, God's chosen people, the bride of Christ, the body of Christ – to name but a few. All of them are imaginatively rich as they evoke Jewish history and contemporary experience. As the body of Christ the Church is to continue his ministry of health and wholeness. It is an imperative that requires a corporate endeavour. Wholeness by its very nature is not achieved by individuals functioning in isolation. Wholeness is the ongoing work of a living organism – the Church.

If we can accept this scenario, and I do not believe we have much choice in the matter if we wish to begin, continue and end faithful to Jesus, then we have gone some of the way to understanding what we must do pastorally in the context of suicide.

If there is any kind of common denominator between those who achieve death by suicide and those who attempt to do so it may be expressed as 'the burden of living has become too great to bear.' There are occasions when all of us find life a burden – times of serious illness, of great disappointment, of unreasonable frustration, of personal rejection. In such times we struggle on. Family and friends support us. The routine of living carries us forward. We eventually win through to a lightening of the load. There are some, however, who do not come out of the tunnel, the light at whose end recedes further and further into the distance. These are those to whom suicide commends itself as a positive release from overwhelming darkness and despair. Is there a possibility that pastoral care can help? I believe there is.

## 5.3    Listening

At the core of being the Church there is a listening function. In order to know what we are to do, we have to learn the mind of Christ by listening to the words of Jesus. That listening involves discernment. These skills of listening and discerning are precisely those that are required to recognise the person on the brink of self-destruction. Within many congregations these skills are blunt and rusty from disuse. We have formally or informally decided that the only person who needs to listen and discern is the minister. Fifteen or twenty minutes of his or her mind delivered from the pulpit on a Sunday are sufficient, we believe, for the rest of us to live by for the remainder of the week. If that is the situation in your church then pastoral care will be thin on the ground and the needs of the person considering suicide will go unrecognised. We in the Church in our ministry of health-giving and wholeness-sustaining have to be engaged in a collective endeavour.

Such an endeavour, to be of any use or value, has to be a non-judgemental one. The person whose interior condition is turning towards self-harm will not be able to begin to unburden himself or herself if the articulated or inarticulated message of the community is that suicide is for one reason or other outside the pale. The person contemplating suicide has to be accepted as a person central to whose personhood is the very fact of the contemplation of suicide. And it is the Church that should especially be able to undertake such acceptance. Why? Because we know we are the ones who are ourselves accepted in and from conditions of equal hellishness by the Father God, who does not require us to do other than recognise our need for forgiveness and acceptance in order to experience his all-embracing love. It is our acceptance by God that impels us in our turn to be the accepting community.

Listening, discerning, accepting, these are the key skills in an individual/corporate ministry of pastoral care for those contemplating suicide. That skill of not judging but accepting is a most important one. It used to be fashionable to try to distinguish between those who are seriously envisaging death by suicide and those who spoke of it or harm themselves as signal sending. The message now is do not begin to try to differentiate. Accept all for what they say themselves to be.

## 5.4    Caring

The question now arises – can the Church move beyond the listening, discerning, and accepting stage of a relationship? Is there more that pastoral care can offer? The answer is most certainly 'Yes'. But before developing that, it is necessary to state emphatically that in any relationship with someone contemplating suicide there is the need to disclose what the real possibilities are of help from other sources. I have been at pains to point out that pastoral care is a corporate activity. Indeed it is, and at its best it will be able to commend and activate the rapidly developing range of diagnostic and support services that exist in our hospitals and healthcare community areas. Psychiatry, psychotherapy and psychological counselling have achieved major sophistication in the help they can offer to those who contemplate suicide. Good pastoral care accepts its own limitations and seeks to identify and commend the sources of help that exist in other institutions and agencies.

Beyond listening, discerning and accepting, there lie other pastoral possibilities. I would identify these as supporting, caring and loving. Listening, discerning and accepting can be described as passive responses and supporting, caring and loving as active. This may be thought to be a trite categorisation but it is one well worth working with for a moment. Those contemplating suicide are almost always in a fragile condition. However, outwardly determined they may appear, their interior is brittle and if not brittle, bruised. Active responses may actually cause more damage, may make the burden that they bear heavier rather than lighter because such responses may suggest that a return response is required. Is there a bridge between the passive and the active, an intermediate state? There is.

## 5.5    Active Support

The community of the Church in New Testament times was significantly differentiated from the rest of the world. It was the place where there was neither Jew nor Gentile, bond nor free, male nor female, young nor old, rich nor poor. It was startlingly different. Our world today is one of frightening competitiveness, suffocating materialism, intense speed, depersonalising isolation, instantaneous non-communication. The Church is invited to defy these dehumanising features of modern life that in combination impel more people towards suicide. It is called upon to defend person-centred living where its sacramental symbols move experience beyond words into realms of mystical reality where there is breath-taking respect for difference and diversity in gender and sex, performance and achievement, poverty and possession, being and doing, as the pilgrimage of the People of God inches closer to that state of total equality that death alone confers on all our beings at this time. For a pastoral ministry to have available a worship experience in community of this order is to have a bridge across that lies the land of support and care and love. Without such a worshipping community a pastoral ministry is entirely dependent on the potential within an individual relationship for a work that is exceedingly demanding, always draining and frequently defeating. Defeating because however constantly available pastoral care has been, and however positively effective it appears to be, suicide will continue to occur. No amount of sustained attention can ever guarantee that someone intent on dying will not do so. That is the stark factual reality that stands at every pastor's shoulder. Neither death nor suicide is yet conquered nor will be until the full and complete realisation of the all-in-allness of Christ.

And so there is the awful, numbing, overwhelming grief of those who are left to mourn – family, friends, acquaintances, yes, and the professional workers, some, perhaps all, of whom will have encountered the person in death rather than in life.

The reality of suicide is often first encountered in the Accident and Emergency Department of a hospital or in its mortuary. Identification may well be required. Sometimes the body is disfigured. Inevitably the coroner will require an autopsy. It is all very traumatic. Those who work in these departments in a hospital find each suicide a new experience of tragedy. They never become immune to the special suffering that each represents. Hospital chaplains play a vital role in providing pastoral support for grieving relatives in the first hours of their bereavement. It is an incredibly difficult task for them. In almost all cases they will not have known the dead person in their life. They are deprived of the conversational intimacies that can be so helpful in other death situations. Yet it is quite extraordinary how often they are able to establish a sustained and sustaining rapport with relatives and friends in their deep distress. In the hospital that I know best, the pastoral care team have established a special ministry of bereavement counselling for those who have experienced the death of a loved one by suicide. People will return time and time again for repeated consolation to the place where grief first came upon them and to the people who stood by them and with them in those first moments of grief. They will join with others who have had the same experiences, to share the pain, mull over the torments, probe the doubts, confess their inadequacies, as they become able to open themselves to the healing caring God in whose own heart is the experience of self-giving dying. The pastoral care provided by a hospital chaplaincy team can be of profound importance in helping folk to begin the process of re-establishing some measure of normality and poise with which to continue living as life goes on as it surely does. The semblance of anonymity in a hospital setting is of immense value in allowing people to come to terms with what has happened. Local congregations should be deeply grateful for such support from the pastors in the hospitals. They are almost always the front-line workers when suicide occurs.

It is, however, in the family church that other contextual issues for future well-being will have to be unpacked. We in Ireland have lived with a culture of secrecy about suicide. That is understandable. While the deed was one of criminal concern it was in fact a matter of profound pastoral conviction that a way should be found not to use the label of suicide. Thank God profoundly that we no longer need to resort to euphemisms or alternative designations. I say 'Thank God profoundly' because if the interior torture of those who have to cope with the suicide of a relative or friend is ever to be eased the matter has to be faced openly. And where better than in the listening, discerning, accepting heart of the Church. I make no apology for the repetition of those profoundly Christ-like attributes for they are the bed-rock of any pastoral care that can be given in these and any other circumstances of deep distress. It is now that the corporate nature of pastoral care becomes fully evident for it will be exercised in so very many different ways. Neighbours will look after children, friends in and outside the local church will rally round with food, folk with the gift of touch will hug and hold and there cannot be too much of it. Those with the gift of tears will shed them so that others, particularly young men, may weep. That quintessential Irish greeting of sympathy, 'I'm sorry for your trouble', takes on a new and deeper and richer meaning and puts words in place where other words fail. And such words can open the door to the other soul-searching speech that aches to be articulated in question after question arising from senses of guilt and shame and anger. 'Why did we not notice?', 'What more could I have done?', 'Why didn't I realise?' And so often, if not always, there was little more that any individual could have done. Behind these questions in the deep recesses of the mind are the shuddering sensations of what the solitary loneliness of dying by suicide must have meant for the person intent on achieving it.

To such questions there are no satisfactory answers. The pastoral response is to allow them to happen and to stand or sit in solidarity of support with all those who must iterate and reiterate their agonies. True pastoral care will exercise a ministry over years. The Church should engage in an endless exercise of loving that affirms and reaffirms the priceless preciousness of one and all established absolutely at Calvary to the end that nothing that God has created can ever be destroyed.

## 5.6    Linking Pastoral Care with Worship

Elsewhere in this book there are words on worship. Let me here write just one or two things. Since 26 per cent of all suicide deaths in the Republic of Ireland are of those under 24 years of age – and the percentage is not dissimilar in Northern Ireland – there is a very special need to be pastoral in the funeral and burial services. In most of our Churches this age group is not easily at home and is decreasingly represented. It is essential that every effort be made to help them to feel at home and to contribute to and share in the worship. Guidance will be needed but it should do no more than refine the natural expressions of esteem, affection, hurt and sorrow. Funerals for this purpose do not need respectability; they have their own inherent authenticity. That authenticity derives from the expression of deep and raw emotion. Such must not be suppressed. God understands. If we cannot be honest about our feelings in his presence, where else can we be honest?

Of course the funeral and burial is only the end of one phase and the beginning of another. In the weeks and months and years that lie ahead pastoral care is going to continue to be of fundamental importance. In these times friendship is what is important. This is true of all bereavements and particularly true in the case of suicide. The offering of friendship can be inhibited by a sense of inadequacy about what we are about to say. Forget it! Just be or rather look to that gracious injunction of Paul to Timothy – ' be given to hospitality' – as a guide. There is ever penetrating insight and constantly unfolding wisdom in the action of Jesus in endowing a meal as the core occasion in which he is to be remembered and celebrated. Hospitality doesn't have to be cordon-bleu or lavish. The simpler the better, at least to begin with, so that without fuss those who mourn experience welcome, acceptance and reincorporation in the processes of life. Allow them to set the pace and discover with them the companionship of silence. Much else will follow in God's good time.

Such a piece as this would be incomplete if it did not reflect on the pastoral care of those who have attempted self-harm and have lived. Do not even consider for one moment the possibility that they never intended to succeed. Such a thought is crassly facile. To try something of the order of suicide with or without succeeding is a signal of the greatest possible significance. It is almost certain that they will be encouraged to seek psychiatric/psychological help. They need such professional help to begin to understand themselves in the context of what they have tried to do to themselves. Pastoral care needs to be extraordinarily sensitive to the professional advice that they are receiving. Conflicting messages can cause great instability. Pastoral care needs to be at the level of affirming them as persons – people with a past who also have a future. All that has been said previously about accepting and not judging applies here with a vengeance. To come back from the near-dead is initially a disorientating experience, joyful for some, depressing for others. So much has to be worked through, particularly if there is a context of close and usually bewildered family. The Church in its ministry of health and wholeness can best provide experience of real stability with a focus on the future about which it knows and understands that the profile of Jesus, that same Jesus, is the best illumination. It is difficult to say more except that prying is absolutely taboo. It is in such circumstances that we in the Church have to learn the difficult lesson that gossip however delicious has no part in pastoral care of this order. Indeed it is almost certain that our pastoral concern and compassion will need to be capable of being exercised in a state of sublime ignorance that is without anything like full knowledge. Friendship does not need to know all before it can be effective.

Those who have tried to care at the coal-face of suicide whether it be for the person himself or herself or parents, relatives, friends need themselves to experience being cared for. Because 'success', whatever that may mean, is never going to be the guaranteed outcome. The sense of failure can be frequent and profound. The Church as the caring community will ensure that the carers are also cared for. Caring in Christ is like a stone thrown into a pond that creates ripples that go on and on until the whole surface, the whole community, is embraced. Let it be so in your Church.

## 5.7    Life

One or two contextual things remain to be said. The presupposition underlying all that has been said is that Life is Gift. Often when that expression is used there is a mental reservation made. Effectively we are saying Life is Gift and Gift it remains until the Giver seeks for its return. I want to ask: is it not of the essence of a gift that once given it becomes the possession of the recipient? Such an understanding seems to be clear in the life and death of Jesus. Calvary would seem to suggest so. Is it unreasonable to pursue this line of thinking further? If my life is my life may I not do what I like with it? When you think about it, most of us live life as if that was a correct assumption. We choose to be selfish or unselfish or, most probably, a highly complex mixture of both. For most of us even our discipleship with Jesus is a tortuous mixture of ambivalence and ambiguity. There is a con-mingling of faith and doubt, certainty and uncertainty. Why then is the act of self-harm so thoroughly excluded from this mix?

I have pondered this question many times. I know that it is a profoundly primitive taboo to set suicide outside the camp because to allow it in would be too disruptive of good social order at the moments when individual and corporate life is most fragile. Such a moment horrendously demonstrated itself in New York and Washington on 11 September 2001 as I was working on this piece. On that same day, some of us were beginning the process of grieving for a good friend whose note of farewell was crystal clear about her intention. It was to relieve those who had the responsibility of caring for her of what she deemed to be a burden too great for them and for herself to bear. Her manner of going was as orderly and distress-free as she could make it. This is by no means the first such instance of its kind in my experience. About her going in our grieving conversations the words noble, courageous, heroic have featured time and time again, and not inappropriately. There are, of course, at the other end of the spectrum suicide experiences so disorderly that they are themselves manifestations of the precipice over which lies chaos and from the edge of which one reels back in horror.

In developing a faithfully pastoral ministry in the name of Christ such variation needs to be recognised and acknowledged so that we may all come to understand that nothing, but nothing, can ever separate us from the love of God that is in Christ Jesus, Our Lord.

# BEREAVEMENT

## 6.1    Introduction

The woman looked hard, grey and shrunken, much older than her sixty years. She wore her grief like a coat of armour, tight and impenetrable. For what seemed an age she said nothing at all; then quietly, and full of anger, the questions began. 'How can you help?' 'How can you understand?' 'What kind of a person are you to make a living out of other peoples' tragedy?' Her words were like daggers seeking to wound, perhaps to kill, as she had been wounded, and as a deep part of her self had been killed with the death of her son.

Gradually, over weeks, as we met regularly, her story began to emerge; her youngest child, her only son, the one in whom she had invested such love and pride and hope, had gone out one evening and had never returned. The Gardaí had found his body a week later. He had died of a massive overdose. Beside the body was a hastily scribbled note bearing just a few words: 'I'm sorry, I can't go on.

Love, Tommy.' It was just after his eighteenth birthday. There seemed to be no explanation for his suicide. Certainly Annie, his mother, could find none. Neither could his friends or family. He had seemed happy in his work, had had lots of friends, and interests. Maybe he'd experimented a bit with drugs, but only in a small way. For Annie the worst part of her situation was the depth of her pain and the strength of her anger. They consumed her every moment 'I didn't know that it was possible to feel such pain and still be alive. Nobody ever told me grief could hurt so much; I'm going mad with it.' She would say this over and over again. The anger came in waves, often threatening to engulf her. Sometimes it was anger with her dead son; sometimes with her family or friends because they didn't or wouldn't try to understand what she was feeling, or because they had children who were still alive. Often it was with God; at times she simply hated God. She was angry with the police, with herself, with everyone.

This anger affected her relationships with others; people withdrew from her because they feared her criticism or her outbursts, and she became isolated and alone with her grief. The other thing that preoccupied her was the constant questioning, the searching for explanations as to why Tommy had killed himself. And then there was the reaction of other people. The family wouldn't speak about Tommy's death at all. Friends and neighbours avoided her. Sometimes when she went into the village shop a silence descended, and instinctively she knew they had all being talking about her, blaming her, she felt, for what had happened. One day she overheard herself being described to a newcomer to the village where her family had lived for generations as 'that suicide's mother'. 'As if nothing else had ever happened to us, as if I'd no other identity,' she commented angrily. Woven through all this was the sense of guilt, exacerbated by the knowledge that it was her sleeping tablets that Tommy had used to end his life. She was plagued with thoughts – if only she had never got the pills, if only she had listened more. No matter what people said she was consumed with the thought that somehow she was to blame for his death. In this miasma of pain and confusion she had existed for five years.

Grief, pain, anger, blame, questioning, vulnerability, social isolation; her experience is not unusual, it encapsulate so much of what is common in the aftermath of suicide. She was not going mad as she so often feared; instead she was dealing with the normal reactions to one of the most difficult situations that any human being has to bear.

## 6.2   Bereavement

In this chapter we will explore what happens when someone is bereaved through suicide. Bereavement is always difficult and each individual's experience is unique and different. Bereavement following a suicide is often particularly painful and tends to be complicated by a number of factors that make it all the more difficult to resolve. For instance, suicide can come apparently 'out of the blue' and thus be very shocking, or it can follow years of argument, trauma, threats, depression and mental illness when family and friends are emotionally worn to nothing and have few resources to call on for this new pain. Suicide can often be very violent. Often there are lots of uncertainties about why the suicide took place and there may be many feelings of guilt. Many people bereaved by suicide feel that friends and colleagues ignore them and dismiss their pain. These are all factors that researchers have found make the healing or resolution of grief more difficult.

Very little in modern life prepares us for the intensity of the pain that is at the core of loss. Sadness is only part of the picture. 'My whole body and soul feel as though they're crying,' said Annie at one stage during our conversations. Our total being is affected and the trauma of loss is experienced at emotional, psychological, physical, spiritual and sometimes sexual levels too. Relationships with other people may become strained. Where death has been very sudden or violent, as is often the case with suicide, there can be a huge sense of shock. When the relationship with the person who dies has been stormy or fraught, this tends to leave a lot of unresolved issues that add to the pain and complexity of grieving. Contrary to popular opinion it is much more difficult to grieve for a difficult or conflicted relationship than for a good one.

Society has changed dramatically in recent years. Our grandparents tended to live in communities that were much more tight-knit. This could often be oppressive, but in situations of crisis such communities were usually supportive. There was also in the past a greater emphasis on extended family offering help or just being there in times of difficulty. People tended to be much more familiar and at home with death and bereavement. There also tended to be time honoured customs with which every one was familiar, everyone knew how to behave or respond in the case of death or tragedy and support was offered freely and naturally to those who were bereaved. Much of this has changed; many people have no contact with death, are very frightened by it, and don't know what to do around bereavement. Thus when death strikes those who are closest are thrown by the intensity of the pain, and frequently those who want to or feel they should offer support don't know what to do, and are tempted to do nothing or run from the situation. This leaves the person who is bereaved feeling isolated as well as traumatised.

Another significant shift are the changes in religious belief and practice that have taken place, with increasing numbers having little or no meaningful connection with organised religion. Thus, when death or trauma strikes, many are deeply bewildered as they have no familiar meaning system with which to make sense of what has happened. The standard rituals of the churches do not necessarily offer relevant spiritual or practical support to this large group. There seem to be few alternatives for them to avail of, and the number of clergy with the time, willingness or skills to develop tailor-made rituals appear to be few. This leads to an increased sense of isolation and lack of support. For these and other reasons those who are bereaved, and most particularly those bereaved through suicide, often find themselves lonely, vulnerable and unsupported.

Bereavement effects the whole person; loss rocks us at emotional, physical, psychological, social, spiritual and sometimes sexual levels too; it effects our relationships, meaning systems and values and it often challenges us to deal with huge change when we feel least able. The purpose of this chapter is to explore the experience of bereavement, particularly bereavement through suicide, and to suggest some guidelines both for those who are going through the experience and those who want to offer real help in such circumstances.

Each individual is unique and all our relationships are quite different; this of course applies to both the living and to the relationships we have had with those who have died. Part of the richness (and the undoubted difficulty) of our connections with others is that they include both the positive and negative, good and not so good elements. The exact configuration of these elements depend on the people involved and the various circumstances and experiences that have been part of the evolution of the relationship. These factors mean that each person (and each family or group) tends to react to loss in a very individualistic way. We also tend to grieve differently for different people, depending on the exact quality of the relationship that has existed. Often the feelings that we experience can seem somewhat contradictory and confusing. When this happens it is useful to remember

FROM DESPAIR TO HOPE

that our emotions, our feelings and our heart are different to our mind's way of working and do not and should not be straitjacketed by logic. The heart has its own sense, its own way.

Don, an only son, had loved his widowed mother very deeply, but he had hated her over-protectiveness towards him. 'It just strangled me,' he observed. When she died, he mourned very deeply, but he also felt profound relief when he could take a girl out without what he described as 'the inquisition'. He would then respond to this sense of relief by feeling guilty, and for a time hid from the guilt by drinking too much and afterwards hating himself for getting out of control. For Don, in his own words, 'My grieving lurches between terrible sadness, freedom, guilt and anger with myself and everyone else.' This is an example of why each person's bereavement experience is highly individualistic and goes some way to explaining why one person may have to cope with more physical symptoms or more guilt, another with more anger and less sadness. Where death has been very sudden or violent there may be more long-term emotional and physical trauma. If the death has happened at a time when an individual or family are having many other difficulties this will also change and perhaps add to the difficulties and complexity of grieving.

Following the death of his father by suicide, John couldn't understand why he was so consumed with anger towards his family. 'I couldn't bear to be with my sisters,' he noted. 'Everyone seemed to expect me to be devastated, but actually I felt very little sadness.' Looking at the relationship that he and his father had had, this made perfect sense. 'My father made my life a quiet hell while he was alive, always in very subtle ways putting me down in front of my sisters, they were on a pedestal. I could never do anything right. A lot of people never really saw what he was at, but I knew. And then he killed himself and left us to pick up the pieces.' After some time he was able to add: 'I don't miss him much at all. I'm sad for the relationship that we never had and I'm still very angry towards him, but I understand now why that is and that it's natural. So I've stopped beating myself up, and I'm not so angry with my sisters, it wasn't their fault.' Sometimes, and at certain stages in the grieving process, it's easier to project our feelings onto someone else, or to disown them completely or to become terribly confused about how we feel or how we should act; this is often the case if we feel the people around won't accept the way we may really feel.

Janet and Victor were deeply committed and highly effective full-time workers with an evangelical missionary organisation. When Victor ended his life, completely out of the blue it seemed, during a period of mild depression at the age of forty-one, Janet was devastated. 'I can't believe he did it; we had so much to live for. I thought I knew him so well, that we shared everything. Now I feel as though I never really knew him at all,' she cried. It felt as though she had been married to a stranger for all those years and that their relationship and sharing had never been real. The sense of closeness and mutual trust that had been central to her sense of their marriage had been torn away. 'How could he have not told me?' She felt as though the God who they had both served so faithfully had cut her off. Often she did not, could not, even believe in Him either. She couldn't stand being with Christian friends, who sought to comfort her with prayer and spiritual encouragement. 'I just can't believe in it all any more,' she often repeated through her tears.

To make matters worse, her efficiency had left her too; she could not concentrate on anything, and had difficulty in even cooking a meal for the children, or in making the simplest decision. Janet had lost her husband at a number of levels; she had also lost her sense of relationship with God. Both had given meaning to her life. She had also lost a deep connection with most of her friends, because she could at least, for the moment, no longer share their reality. And she had also lost her sense of herself as an efficient, coping person Trying to find consolation and emotional comfort she lurched from one passionate sexual relationship to another. Janet sensed that many of her former friends and colleagues were withdrawing from her, they could not understand the new person whom she had become. 'They're praying over me in public and discussing me in private, like I was a scarlet woman. Maybe I am,' she sobbed. In many ways she shared their bewilderment; she did not understand or know this new person; everything seemed unfamiliar and terribly frightening. Her normal supports and structures had dissolved. It took time for Janet to emerge into a new place of peace and confidence, but she ultimately managed that transition, with the non-judgemental support and care of a group of others bereaved by suicide.

Deep or traumatic loss may, at times, have such an effect, changing our whole way of seeing the world, both past and present, our relationships and our sense of self. This is a deeply perturbing experience, but is also a normal part of grief

As can be seen from the above descriptions the pain of bereavement is made up of a number of distinct strands, weaving in and out of each other like a dark tapestry, and varying greatly from person to person depending on a wide range of variables. Despite some views to the contrary, these threads do not follow any particular order, and they take their own time to heal; they rarely fall into neat categories. We will now focus a little more detail on the most significant of these strands – particularly as they apply to suicide bereavement.

## 6.3    The Grief Experience: (a) Feelings and Emotions

The most commonly recognised feeling connected with grief is sadness. However, there are a range of other feelings that are just as much a part of grief. Guilt, anger, shock, anxiety and depression are perhaps the most significant of these. People can also feel very isolated and alone. In suicide there can be the added burden of not knowing exactly why the person took their life. There can also be lots of fears for the future, questioning of values, and disruption of relationships. Well-meaning friends, and at times professionals, have tried to either deaden these feelings in one way or another or else to distract those who are bereaved from what they are really experiencing, believing that they were thus easing the pain. However, the healing and resolution of grief tends to be through experiencing such feelings rather than by avoiding or by-passing them. Allowing the person to stay with and explore their feelings of sadness, guilt, anger or depression is a far more effective and precious gift. This is particularly so in the case of suicide, where feelings may be very intense, of long duration and all the more in need of venting.

## Sadness
Sadness is often (but not always) a most significant companion of loss and usually expresses itself through tears, feelings of heaviness, sighs, dreams, at times a sense of greyness that seems to tinge everything, and through a deep preoccupation with the person who has died. While the sadness may focus mainly on the person who has gone, it is in a very real way connected to ourselves as well. 'I feel that part of me has gone too, or I feel as though half of my body is missing now,' are phrases that are often heard from those who have experienced bereavement. In a strange but very powerful way we loose part of ourselves when someone close to us dies and we mourn for that loss too. When her Mum, to whom she had been very close, died, Jenny felt as though she had also lost a central part of herself. 'There were things that Mum knew about me, there were parts of me that no one else knew or will ever know in the same way; I feel that they

have gone now, its as if I have to be a different person.'

When death occurs through suicide survivors often feel, as Janet did, that they never really knew the person at all, and this can result in their feeling that they have lost not just the physical person, but that they have been robbed or cheated out of the past relationship, with its stories, shared memories and richness. Sadness may also be about the future, grieving the loss of what might have been, a career, grandchildren or a future together.

Sadness will not always be present and it will not always be visible or manifest in predictable ways. Eventually the sadness tends to become somewhat more bearable; 'Its not that its gone, there's still a huge void, a deep pain, but its become part of me, its kind of more liveable with, and I can sometimes laugh and forget for a little time,' said Annie after some months of counselling. Sadness may persist as a central part of a person's life for many years. Even when it has lessened to some degree, it can hit the individual (or indeed group) out of the blue and at the most unexpected moments and in a most overpowering way. It may well be particularly strong around anniversaries, birthdays, holiday times, Christmas or at other significant occasions.

When sadness does not appear to be present this may be so for four main reasons:

i   because it is actually not there for some reason, e.g. relief that the deceased person's pain is finished;

ii  because it is so profound that it is impossible for the person to easily 'get at';

iii because the person does not feel they have permission to express it, or;

iv  perhaps because another, stronger emotion or need has replaced it.

When his wife died by suicide, after a long illness, Walter was so busy looking after the couple's four grief-stricken young children, he felt he had to put his sadness 'on hold'. In any case 'if I had space to express any emotion, it would be anger because she left me with such a mess,' he said on a number of occasions. Sometimes a sense of relief may be more profound than anything else, perhaps because the deceased's suffering is at an end or because the relationship was so fraught and this is now at an end; this is quite normal. In other situations the sense of shock may be so strong that it takes over, or the sadness may be so deep for a time as to be inexpressible through tears or talking and may thus manifest itself through illness or physical symptoms instead. When his father died in his arms, Martin, aged sixteen, as the oldest child, immediately took on the job of caring for his devastated mother and younger siblings. He was so busy providing for and supporting the family that he did not attend to his own sadness until some twenty years later when, by now a father himself, he was diagnosed with Rheumatoid Arthritis. Only then in a session with a hospital social worker did his long frozen grief break out and he cried solidly for three days. 'I wonder did my sadness somehow get trapped inside my body and turn into Arthritis?' he wondered after this explosion.

In another situation Jonathon's younger brother Dermot, had been diagnosed with Schizophrenia when he was fourteen and increasingly suffered from an appalling quality of life. At the age of twenty-four he found the present too difficult and the future too horrific to contemplate, (drug treatment had not managed to control his condition), and he took his own life. After an initial period of shock, Jonathon, who had for some years been living in Asia, and had developed a rather different view of life and death to that which was common in Ireland, felt huge relief that Dermot's pain was over. He also experienced a sense of profound admiration for what he saw as his brother's bravery in ending his pain. When Jonathon shared of these feelings at the funeral service, his family reacted violently, rejecting his views and rejecting him in what he experienced as a most hurtful way. While their reaction came from a deep sense of hurt and perhaps from the pain and frustration of Dermot's years of suffering, their reaction devastated Jonathon. Ten years later the situation remains largely unresolved.

*Guilt*

Guilt can be almost overpowering for those who have been bereaved, and particularly for those who have been bereaved by suicide. Individuals blame themselves for the death, or for not being caring enough for the person who has died, or for having been impatient or unresponsive to the needs and wants of that person. Sometimes guilt may be a realistic response, the outcome of a poor relationship; frequently however, it is unrealistic. In either instance it is important for the bereaved person to be allowed to feel, experience, talk about, explore and process this sense of guilt. It is only in doing so that they can ultimately let it go and move on.

In the context of suicide guilt tends to be a very significant force. Because the cause for suicide is frequently very unclear, survivors can become preoccupied with blaming themselves, saying 'if only I had listened more or been more available, or if only I had not been impatient, or if only I hadn't gone out this might not have happened.' While this is a natural reaction and people need to be allowed to explore and speak of their guilt in order to move beyond it, it is important in the last analysis to recognise that suicide is not a reaction to one or two instances. It is instead the culmination of a whole series of events, the ending of a long roadway, often marked by much pain and difficulty, whether or not this was visible to those around.

Those who take their life through suicide will often have gone to a lot of effort to hide their intention from those at hand. They may also have felt unable because of constraints within themselves to share their true feelings with others.

## Anger

Anger is an important part of bereavement for many. This anger may be towards the person (for dying), towards friends or family members (for all sorts of things), towards professionals involved (for not being supportive or effective or caring), or towards God (often for not preventing the situation). Some of the reasons for the anger will be quite logical or reasonable, others less so. In either instance people need to be allowed, and encouraged to express their anger. This can be an important part of the healing of grief. Christians have tended to be uncomfortable around anger (their own and other peoples) and indeed at times, and in some circles, around the expression of any emotion. Anyone who reads the Psalms will realise how at home David was with a full and free expression of anger and all the other range human emotions. He is frequently very angry with God, as well as with his fellows, and in both instances states this, sometimes quite explosively. He does not in any way either hide or censor his anger and in the process of expressing it seems to move beyond it. Grief counsellors tend to agree with him. Express it, don't swallow it, is the message.

There is a strong temptation for those who are trying to support the bereaved, and indeed for the bereaved person themselves, to become pre-occupied with whether the anger is reasonable or not; this is irrelevant; its much more productive to encourage its expression – reasonable or not! If it feels real for the person it is real! What the supporter needs to do is give a space for its expression; they don't have to feel the same way themselves. It is not appropriate to get involved in justifying or trying to explain away the situation or behaviour that is causing the anger. Only in such supportive contexts can bereaved people be allowed to express, explore and ultimately let go of the hurt that invariably lies at the root of anger.

It is also important to recognise that anger is a powerful force for creating change. Many of the great movements for social change and for the promotion of justice and equality in society have been motivated and fuelled by anger that has been clearly focused. For instance some of the appalling practices common until quite recently in many Irish hospitals following stillbirth have been changed because of the anger of bereaved parents who made representations at local and political levels, insisting that such systems be changed and humanised. At a different level Martin Luther King was motivated by anger in his crusade to change segregation and discrimination in the Deep South of America. The energy of anger can be used to create positive change, and we have only to look at the prophets of the Old Testament to see that much of their motivation for creating social and spiritual change came from anger.

It is always important, while accepting that anger may be an emotional reaction, to also take it seriously, and to look at the wider situation. Frequently the focus of anger may be extremely valid. Professionals do make dreadful mistakes for which they need to take responsibility. The legal system often puts huge added and unnecessary strain on bereaved families. There is need for huge change. The Church and its representatives have often been part of creating additional misery, particularly around suicide, magnifying and exacerbating the pain of those who are bereaved by culpable insensitivity, poor pastoral practice and dubious ritual. Only in the expression and heeding of anger can pressure be brought to bear to create change.

## Depression

The grey pall of depression, where life has lost energy, hope, interest and stimulation is often the companion of grief. It is extremely trying to live with. It is also very trying for those friends or relations who are seeking to offer support. Nothing seems to help. Some theorists suggest that depression comes about through anger that is unexpressed becoming unconsciously turned inwards by the person on themselves. Others suggest that it is sadness that has become frozen. Both psychiatry and psychology, as well as other disciplines, make a distinction between Reactive Depression, which is a response to a particular situation or set of situations, and Endogenous Depression which is of a deeper nature. In cases where depression is significant it is important to seek professional help and medication, as well as counselling, which can be of real assistance. Depression is not something to hide or of which to be ashamed. It is a real human experience and our Christian faith encourages us to be real and to acknowledge what is going on for us, no matter how difficult this may be. Usually it is only in doing so that we can begin to move forward on the journey of healing.

Anger, guilt, depression and sadness are all emotions that people in twenty-first-century society find it difficult to be around. We shy away from such feelings unlike our forebears, and many so called 'under developed' peoples, who had or still have, the skill of staying with and encouraging the expression of feeling (if this is what the bereaved person finds appropriate). We tend to be more comfortable diverting bereaved people from such feelings, offering distraction, tea or alternatives activities. All these do have their place. However, majoring all the time on distractions may not be helpful as this tends to give the message that we do not wish people them to be real at a feeling level or to share with us in this way. This in turn discourages emotional expression and can slow or prevent healing.

Not everyone finds it easy to talk about their loss, and people's differences and difficulties need to be respected. What is important to convey is that the person is accepted as they are and as they feel at a particular time. Conveying the acceptability of talking about the loss, of tears, of anger or whatever else seems appropriate is important.

It's central for the bereaved to find spaces that balance talking, silence, distraction, emotional support or activity. Sensitive common sense is a good guide as well as asking the person what they themselves feel might be helpful and being guided by this. Crying with the person, deep sharing, a prayer meeting, a social outing, a walk, a drinking session, all have their places depending on the individuals involved.

Feelings, and their expression or indeed their non-expression, can become mixed together in a highly volatile cocktail; add relationships to this mixture and the reality that people are both raw, vulnerable and highly sensitive at such times as this further underlines the potential for difficulty.

If feelings are not expressed directly they may become changed into another emotion or 'projected' onto someone else entirely. Both seemed to happen when Janet, the former missionary began her sexual adventures, leaping into bed with a succession of men and women and then abandoning them. With hindsight she realised that she may have been indirectly expressing her anger towards both God and Victor for abandoning her. Perhaps if she had been given the non-judgemental support she needed so much, she might not have had to go to such extremes to express her anger indirectly.

## 6.4 The Grief Experience: (b) Changes and Troubled Waters

The feeling and emotional reactions are so much part of bereavement that it is easy to forget that there are other very significant parts of the experience that can be just as troubling. Loss is such a deep perturbation that it can create changes in us at almost all levels of our being. What is happening at a feeling level also feeds into other areas of our experience creating a pool of troubled waters that can be very difficult to manage. We now look at some of these areas.

## Relationships

After a death it goes without saying that everyone is vulnerable. At such times the support and understanding of others may feel particularly important. However, at such times it often feels as though others just don't provide the support that we need. Sadly it is at this very time that people often experience difficulty or indeed break-up in friendships and significant relationships. Research, for instance, indicates that many marriages break down after the death of a child. There are a number of reasons that help explain why such things happen. Because our feelings lie so deep and are quite confused, it may be very difficult to express in words what we are really experiencing. And we may also fear that what we really feel is not what we should be feeling or what others would expect us to feel. Our feelings may also lurch in very unpredictable and contradictory ways and in ways that we find it impossible to explain to ourselves let alone to others. Because of all this our communication with others can tend to be very unclear, which makes it hard for them to relate to us and get a clear understanding of what is going on or of what we may need.

Frequently, because no guidelines exist in our society for supporting the bereaved, people neither know what to do or what to say. They are afraid of saying the wrong thing or of making the situation even worse and so they withdraw or avoid the survivor. Sometimes this avoiding behaviour is for a deeper reason. People are very frightened by death, and being in contact with the bereaved reminds them graphically of their own mortality, or of that of their loved ones. It can also emphasise the awfulness of the pain of bereavement. For others, connecting with a bereaved person reminds them too powerfully of their own loved ones who have died. In either instance the temptation is to avoid the bereaved person or the subject of death, effectively shielding themselves from pain and distress, but at the same time giving a very clear message to the bereaved that raising the subject of the loss is taboo.

As already mentioned people grieve differently and at different rates. Men and women also cope with loss in very different ways. While this is both natural and healthy, it can cause problems in families and amongst groups of friends. This is particularly so because there is a spoken or unspoken expectation that family members, or a group of friends, should be able to offer each other mutual support. This is rarely realistic. When Mary and Paul's fourteen-year-old son John died by suicide, Mary was inconsolable; after some months she became deeply depressed. She could talk of nothing but her dead son. She could not understand how Paul went back to work so quickly and became immersed in it, how he always wanted to be on the move and how he rarely mentioned their boy. To her it seemed as though Paul did not care, that he must never have loved their son. She also felt very rejected because Paul did not spend time with her or ask how she felt. It seemed to her as though she had never really known her husband.

Gradually they grew further and further apart. Paul felt this and sensed Mary's rejection of him, and gradually began to deeply resent it, feeling that she should have trusted him and understood that his pain was so deep that he could not bear to speak of John; that he immersed himself in his work in a fruitless attempt to distract himself from the pain. He could not bear to listen to his wife or even to spend time with her because she spoke of nothing but their loss. He felt that surely she could have reached out to him or even to their other children. To him her pre-occupation with the dead seemed to be a rejection of the living. Their non-communication turned to anger and ultimately to hatred and separation. They had very different styles of grieving, and had an unspoken expectation that the other would understand and be available. Given the depth of their loss and their inability to communicate at a feeling level, this was a disastrous combination. Perhaps an outsider, or neutral professional would have offered the individual support that was needed, helped each to clarify what was going on for the other, and ultimately aided them to communicating this with the other.

Anger, rejection and the need to punish are often, as we have noted, a central part of the grieving process. Such emotions are difficult to be around at the best of times. Often others, friends or colleagues, take such responses as personal reactions or rejections and react in return, rather than understanding that the bereaved person just needs to vent these emotions and that they are not personal. Its then that relationships begin to crack. Christians, including 'professional' Christians such as ministers or leaders, are often not good at staying with such expressions and either contradict or justify or withdraw. The bereaved individual is then left with the unsatisfactory choice of censoring their feeling and resenting this, or of expressing their feeling and risking rejection, correction or platitudes. The expression of negative emotion is quite natural and it does not necessarily mean personal rejection. Because of all these 'dynamics' it is very difficult for family members or friends who have shared a relationship with the deceased to offer each other huge amounts of support.

Our society is not very good at handling death or bereavement issues, and this means that many people, from embarrassment or fear, do not offer real support. While it may be either hurtful or disappointing, it is important for those who have been bereaved not to take this personally or as a reflection on themselves. Sometimes it can be helpful to actually tell people or remind them (if you feel you can do this) what you need in the way of support – they don't have crystal balls, and if you don't say they won't automatically know! You may also need to accept that some friends, relations and indeed

FROM DESPAIR TO HOPE

professionals are just not going to be able to offer the support you need.

*Spiritual Issues*

This is a very wide area and includes a number of strands that weave together to make up a significant part of the bereavement experience. First of all there are the reactions that are connected to spirituality in a traditional sense, for instance a deepening of faith or alternatively a feeling of meaninglessness around prayer and churchgoing. Or a questioning of what we had always accepted. Secondly there may be a change in our values or our way of seeing the world. Our priorities may be turned on their head. Lastly, many bereaved people have strange or unusual experiences that they have not had before, for instance seeing or having a very profound sense of the presence of the one who has died, or at times seeing or hearing that person. Some find this deeply comforting; others are frightened. What is important to remember is that these experiences are perfectly natural and are as much a part of bereavement as sadness.

After a death, the world is turned upside down; suddenly what we felt to be secure and normal is turned on its head. Everything seems confused and unreal. Because something as dramatic and perturbing as the death of a loved one has occurred everything may seem up for grabs and we suddenly begin to question the relevance or reliability of much of what we had previously relied upon. We may find ourselves questioning beliefs, values, relationships and activities. This can feel like a huge added burden. We want certainty, for things to be as they were, and all we find is a sense of uncertainty or perhaps emptiness. If a loved one has died tragically we may begin to doubt the reliability and the love of others and of God. As a deeply spiritual deacon of a strict Baptist congregation said, following the tragic death of his wife, 'The Heavens were like brass for me; I felt I had been abandoned by Him too; I could not experience His love. Although I continued to pray, read the Bible and attend the services and prayer meetings, I might as well have sat out in the middle of the road, for all the meaning they had.' Another woman who had always strongly believed in the right of people to take their own life reacted with confusion and questioning of her own values when her sister died by suicide.

Sadness and a sense of depression colour everything. This is natural. It's important not to deny, even to oneself, that such feelings are real. Trying to force oneself to belief does not usually work. Instead it may be important to find someone to share with, who will listen and respect what is being said and felt, as well as what cannot be spoken. It may also be useful to find what does nurture or comfort or speak to you spiritually. This will vary greatly from person to person. For one it may be attending a completely different form of service, for another it may be just resting in the reality of what you are feeling; for another it may be playing a piece of music, going for a country walk and observing the colours, or it may be in doing something just for you. In time things will settle down. This may not be to return to what you were or to what you did believe, but rather, when the time is right and you have the energy, to move on to what you can become and to what you can believe and value.

There is also another range of experiences often described as 'spiritual' in the wider sense of this word, and in a way that would not always be seen as accurate in Christian circles. Whatever these are called, it is very important to recognise these as normal to loss. Such experiences can include seeing the person who has died, hearing their voice, or sensing their presence; there may also be very vivid dreams, perceived messages or quite extraordinary series of coincidences. These are all quite normal, and are a very common part of grief, even if we don't always know quite how to explain them. When such things happen some people feel that they are going quite mad. Others see these experiences as a gift and find huge comfort in them. Others wish they could have them and can't. Perhaps the most useful reaction is to allow such events to help you in whatever way seems appropriate. Remember there are more things in heaven and earth than any of us can fully explain.

An elderly woman whose late husband had been a very committed pipe smoker all their married life (much to her irritation) was at first puzzled some months after his death, and then alarmed by the aroma of fresh tobacco smoke that she found every evening in her sitting room. She lived alone and was not a smoker herself. Eventually she found this experience very comforting, feeling that her husband was letting her know that he was keeping an eye on her.

Something else that people worry about is the fate of the person who has died by suicide. Often those with little or no Church connection may have worries in this area. Visions of hell may leap to mind or perhaps exist at an unspoken level. Frequently it's hard to put these worries into words and so sensitive and imaginative pastoring becomes important. Past attitudes to suicide, together with stories of the bodies of those who have died through suicide being refused burial in consecrated ground often add to these concerns. In this context it may be important to point out that no outright condemnation of suicide can be found anywhere in the Bible. Gods love is very deep and full of understanding and reaches out to everyone, particularly to people in their pain, need or confusion.

*Behaviours*
Our world is turned upside down by death, and practically everything that we think, see, say or do is affected. Emotions, physical health, values, family connections, our standing in the community may all be touched. The way that we see both others and ourselves is changed for better

or worse. This in turn dramatically affects our behaviour. For some it becomes impossible to do things that were previously easy; others have just no interest or enjoyment in what they had always liked in the past. Change, confusion, and the inability to concentrate or relate are all a natural part of grief.

George was the managing director of a large multi-national company. When his wife died after a long and painful illness he at first coped very well. He had nursed, cared for and supported his wife through her illness, and his main feeling on her death was relief that her pain was over. When he returned to work, at first he was full of energy. Then little by little he began to have more and more difficulty functioning, decision making became impossible. Then his colleagues began suggesting that he should be back to normal. This made things worse and eventually he found himself spending each day paralysed, able only to move papers from one side of his desk to the other. He thought that he was going mad and eventually became quite suicidal. It never struck him that all this was part of his bereavement until his GP reminded him of all that he'd been through.

Sometimes because people see things very differently following bereavement and because their world has been turned upside down they will behave in ways that are unusual for them, as Janet did after Victor's death. Others find it simply impossible to perform the every day tasks demanded by work, family or relationships, and become upset and perturbed by this. Those who are bereaved, particularly those who are bereaved through suicide are generally in trauma, and this trauma may continue for a long time. Support, kindness, and understanding are all important. Most important of all is the need for the individuals involved to be supported in caring for themselves and to be helped to realise the normality of what they are going through.

*Physical Effects*

Grief is so big that it makes sense to recognise that the body also reacts in a variety of ways to what has happened. Some researchers feel that shock affects the smooth working of the immune system and that following a bereavement, the immune system's functioning becomes depressed, and so the body is much more open to infection. This would certainly explain why physical health is often quite bad following a death. Many people complain of colds, flues, sore throats, migraines, back ache and feelings of just being very under the weather. Changes in sleep patterns either needing much more sleep or being unable to sleep despite profound tiredness are common experiences. Sometimes too there are more dramatic and serious episodes of illness requiring hospitalisation; it is as if the body is trying not only to come to terms with the death, but also to express its sense of outrage at what has happened. Feelings of deep heaviness in the chest area, tightness in the throat, a sense of great weight in various limbs are all common physical side effects. If someone has a chronic condition anyway, such as a bad back or other 'weak' point, this will often play up, as if the body is registering its protest through a familiar route.

Recognising that physical vulnerability is part of bereavement is an important first step to take. The idea of 'listening to my body' may be one that it is important to get used to. Instead of 'pushing' to do more, a better idea may be to respect a symptom – tiredness, pain or infection, and to listen openly to whether it is saying – to ease up, or to rest, or to take a break. Try this instead of pushing the body and ignoring pain or tiredness or illness. Sometimes symptoms have to become worse before they are heard or attended to. Listening to the body is not easy and only happens with practice; being sensitive to what it is saying, learning to attend to its messages, rather than seeing these as negatives that must be fought against, takes practice but yields great benefits.

At times others do not help either by encouraging the bereaved person to get back to their normal activities too soon. There needs to be a balance between returning to normality and holding on to space to grieve. In busy twenty-first century lives sometimes we only give ourselves time to be with our grief in the way we really need to when the body shouts so loudly that it cannot be ignored.

### Isolation and Stigma

Following his wife's death C.S. Lewis spoke of the isolation he experienced as a bereaved person. 'I'm aware of being an embarrassment to every one that I meet ... perhaps the bereaved ought to be isolated in special settlements like lepers.' He was giving voice to a very common experience that is often accentuated when the bereavement has been through suicide.

This sense of isolation has two forms; firstly an internal isolation in which an individual feels completely numbed and cut off from others by the awfulness of what has happened. It feels as if no one else could possibly understand or reach through the pain in any real way. In such circumstances withdrawal may seem to be the only option that seems possible. The second form of social isolation often goes hand in hand with this, where people find that friends, colleagues, neighbours are treating them differently to before, or are not connecting with them or including them. As we noticed earlier this may be because others do not know what to do, or because they are so afraid of death that they avoid the situation completely. This makes the pain of bereavement worse.

Recent research also indicates that shame appears to be a significant part of suicide bereavement, where family and friends feel in some way odd and different because of what has happened. 'It feels as though there must have been something deficient about me as a parent, or at least with our family for this to have happened,' noted Jean following the suicide of her fifteen year old son.

Some survivors fear that the person who has taken their own life must have been rejecting them or their values at a very deep level. 'It feels as though there must have been something very wrong with me, with us and with how we lived and he saw it. And then I see people looking at me in the street or in the shop and I feel that that's what they're thinking too. Maybe what I'm picking up from others my is imagination gone wild, but if I'm having a bad day it feels so real,' said Mary as she wondered about how she was coping after her daughter had killed herself. 'I'm terrified of having another close loving relationship and yet it's what I most long for. But I feel as though I'm not worthy, that I could never be wanted for me. I'm terrified that the same thing might happen again,' explained a young widow some years after her husband had taken his life.

In some mysterious way it is as if survivors are experiencing in their own lives and relationships the traditional stigma associated with suicide. In such situations they may withdraw and isolate themselves, making it difficult for others to offer support or care. This can result in the bereaved individuals or families feeling themselves becoming more and more alone which in turn compounds the experience of 'difference' or stigma.

Close and supportive relationships that allow bereaved people to come to value and trust themselves afresh are deeply important in the healing of these particular facets of grief after suicide.

## Why? – Trying to Understand

Trying to come to terms or trying to understand why a death has happened is part of all bereavement. In some cases of suicide the reasons may be very clear to those who remain. 'I know he just couldn't take any more,' said Derek after his son's death following years of mental illness. At times, however, the reasons will be unclear, contradictory or sometimes quite mysterious. Or what makes complete sense as an explanation to one family member makes no sense at all to another.

Often those who are bereaved are left groping, going round in circles and torturing themselves in the search for clues or answers. These may or may not exist. But the urge to search is very strong. A seventy year old widow whose husband had died by suicide over forty years ago illustrates the pain and frustration of this search. 'I still don't know why he did it. For years, I'd say for well over thirty years, I went round and round in circles. It went round and round in my head...Why? Why? Why? It was like being addicted. I used to go to his grave and scream 'WHY?' at him. I went to mediums, psychologists, priests, anyone. I still don't know, but somehow now I've gradually let go of needing an answer ... it made sense to him at the time, that's all I know, and I suppose I'll just live with that.' The questions are endless. Often they're to the person who has died. Or to oneself. Why didn't you just speak to me, tell me what was going on for you? Where did I go wrong? If I had done something differently would that have made a difference? If she'd gone to a different school? What's wrong with my family? Why are people so uncaring? The list goes on and on.

Often at the root of the questioning is a sense of guilt. 'How can I ever know that it wasn't my fault if I don't know why she did it,' sobbed Joan on the second anniversary of her daughter's death. Sometimes there may be a need to blame others. 'I think it was the way he treated her that was the last straw, but unless I actually know I can't really blame him; maybe it wasn't. I'm so confused,' Joan said on another occasion as she talked about her son-in-law. Perhaps the hardest part of all this is that the person who has died cannot be asked for an explanation. This being the case some survivors are helped by finding out as much as they possibly can about the person who has gone, recognising that at best no matter how well we know the person our knowledge is partial. Seeking the perspective of friends or professionals or by reading around the growing area of suicide motivation can be useful. Sharing with others who have been bereaved is sometimes helpful. And recognising that this is a normal part of loss is important.

Edith's husband took his own life in the nineteen-fifties, when he was thirty and she a year younger, leaving her with four young children to raise. 'I spent years asking why, blaming myself, blaming him, blaming his mother, going in circles. It wasn't until I was in my seventies that I resolved to try and leave no stone unturned. Northern Irish society had changed by then and I felt maybe there were some clues that I had previously overlooked. Eventually I was able to contact an old friend and confidante of my husband's, while I was visiting my daughter in Australia. He had left Ireland just after John's death. I'd always wondered about that ... and he was so upset at the funeral. He confirmed what I was beginning to suspect. John had apparently had questions about his sexual orientation since he was very young. Of course such things weren't spoken of much at the time.

'Apparently he went for help to two highly respected clergymen in our denomination; he was condemned out of hand by the first of them, told that he was a disgrace to his family and that he was in danger of committing the unforgivable sin. The other told him to "trust in God, find a nice Christian girl, and get married." I think I was the nice Christian girl. Of course I was angry with John for not talking to me, but then I realised that I wouldn't have understood and the Church and the clergy had such power then. The rest of us didn't have a clue.

'I'm so sad, he was such a lovely man. I know now his pain must have been unbearable. They did that to him, the society of the time, the Church; they did that to me, to my children. God forgives them; I'm afraid I can't ... not yet anyway, though I do pray and pray for help. At least now I think I understand; the "whys" have stopped. And there are still some questions I've never asked. It all still hurts so much.

'You know I've been a committed Christian since I was thirteen. I love my Saviour and so did John. But I haven't been able to set my foot over a church threshold since I worked out what really happened. What makes it worse is that no one from my church has even called to ask why I've stopped attending.'

Edith died recently; her minister gave a most moving eulogy at the funeral. Her Church commitment was praised, and her recent lack of attendance was excused on grounds of 'poor health'. Her husband's death was not even referred to.

*Suicidal Intent*

Suicidal thoughts are quite common among those who have been bereaved; sometimes it is a desire to be re-united with the person who has died that is the cause; sometimes it is because life feels so empty and arid; sometimes such feelings are linked to depression. Such thinking can take the form of actively thinking about taking one's own life; equally it may be just a complete indifference to dying. 'I couldn't care less if I died tomorrow,' said Annie as she processed the death of her son. Alternatively, some survivors will involve themselves either actively or passively (for instance through physical neglect) in dangerous or quite self-destructive and life-threatening behaviours.

When a suicide has taken place, this can make a previously unconsidered or unthinkable option a possibility for others. Suicide can suddenly appear as a potential solution to problems in a way that it never had before. This to some degree accounts for the high level of 'copy-catting' that has been observed particularly among young people following the death through suicide of a friend, relation or member of their peer group. This reality underlines the need for supportive and caring relationships in which the bereaved person can feel safe, respected and cared for in their pain, and on the long journey towards recovery. It also points to the advisability of people being taught to be aware of their own potential and the importance of self-empowerment as a crucial element in educational and community programmes. It is essential for churches and other 'caring organisations' to own their responsibility as potential creators of pressure for social and political change. Many suicides take place because people of all ages feel that they have no other realistic possibilities and this is why one suicide in a group or area can promote many others to think along the same lines.

## 6.5    Responding to Bereavement

*If you have been bereaved by suicide*
If you have been bereaved through suicide you may recognise some of the experiences that we have been noticing in this chapter. You may have connected with some of the people whose stories have been glimpsed. You may have seen something of their feelings or circumstances reflected in your own pain or anger, isolation or confusion. Ed Dunne, an American counsellor and psychotherapist, notes that the death by suicide of a younger brother utterly changed his life; many years later he is still deeply effected by the experience. Another counsellor who since her son's suicide has devoted much of her life to working with those who are survivors, speaks of the profound sense of isolation, and the sense of deep vulnerability that she feels. She shares too the huge sense of stigma that she experienced as the mother of her son.

There is little doubt that the suicide of a loved one is one of the most profoundly painful experiences that life can ever throw up. There are no magic wands that bring quick or easy healing, comfort or resolution. Instead there is a journey or a roadway. The journey is neither short, direct or straight. There are many bends and dips and hills on the roadway. Sometimes, perhaps when you feel least able, the roadway disappears and you are left somehow to create your own path. Often it may be that the journey is moving in circles and after huge effort you find yourself back almost where you started. Often the journey will take you through terribly bleak and lonely landscapes and very rough terrain. That is probably the reality.

However there will also be some supports or helps along the way. Perhaps some of these will appear when you least expect them, others you may have to be responsible for finding for yourself. Sometimes the countryside through which you pass will appear fertile and comforting and nurturing and sometimes you may just have to put energy into making it so. In this process some of the following may be of help.

a) Lower your expectations of yourself. Remember that you are on a long and very difficult roadway; let go of what you don't need or what is not helpful; you don't need excess heavy baggage on this journey. Don't expect too much of yourself. Grief is difficult enough – so don't torture yourself. In all probability you will not be able to do a lot of the things that you were previously able to do at least for the present. Or you may not even wish to. Give yourself time.

Find ways to be good to yourself, to take care of yourself. Don't waste your energy when you have it, nurture it with care. When you have to do something, try to choose some things that you find life-giving as well as the every-day drudgery.

And when the pain is there try not to fight it or avoid it. Instead, go with it and attend to it as a companion; if you listen to it will be able to tell you how much of how you need to support and care for yourself.

b) Be conscious of who you could or do get help from. Be realistic. No matter how much you wish them to or no matter how much they should be able to, some people just do not seem able to give what is needed, and it tends to be a waste of time and energy expecting or trying to make them do so. This goes not only for family, friends and neighbours but also for professionals. Be aware that some people are just too close to you or the situation to be of much help; this may include your partner, parents, siblings or closest friends. Your family may also be grieving. If they are, because people grieve in different ways and at different rates and have very different needs, you may not be of much use to them nor they to you. Tell them what's going on for you and listen if you can non-judgementally to them, but don't expect too much. Instead put energy into finding other sources of support, at least for the moment.

And consider: what support would be most useful for you from others? What can you do that would most help them to give this?

c) Try to be aware of what you need or what would be of most help and remember to look at emotional, physical, psychological and spiritual levels. Again be realistic. People need very different things at different stages of their journey and sometimes this varies from one day to the next. Many people have found a lot of support through counselling, bereavement groups, alternative medicine, aromatherapy or massage. There is also art, music, nature, new or different voluntary or paid work, perhaps different relationships or interest groups. When you feel ready there are possibilities. Support does exist out there and at some stages it may be helpful to experience the distraction and stimulation of doing new things; being with new people. At other times you need the old, familiar and predictable. If you have the energy don't be afraid to experiment to see what works for you.

And don't be afraid to say 'no'; sometimes in their anxiety to help 'get you back to normality' or to avoid dealing directly with pain (yours or their own) people can be very pressurising.

*If you are supporting someone who has been bereaved through suicide*
If on the other hand you find yourself seeking to accompany another even for a while on their journey of suicide bereavement you need to be aware that it is not something to be undertaken lightly. Equally realise that it is sometimes the smallest gestures – the call, the invitation – that mean the most. This sometimes needs to be realised by professionals as well as everyone else.

Be prepared to learn many things – mainly about yourself. You will also need to be prepared to learn or improve some skills. Learning the art of sensitive and imaginative anticipation of where the other person may be at at a particular time, emotionally, psychologically, physically or spiritually, is very important. You will need to hone your skills in how to respond appropriately in such contexts. Jeffry Zurheide, an American Baptist pastor and hospital chaplain, invites those who are setting out on such journeys of support to 'Bow your spirit as you enter'. Be respectful even if you don't understand. Be prepared to be vulnerable, to not have the right answers, often to have no answers. Most of the time answers are meaningless in the face of tragedy and loss. It is far better to say 'I don't know' rather than to embark on a theological or philosophical thesis or worse to hide behind banalities. Realise that you are not going to take away the pain of the other. You have no magic wands at your disposal; what you may be able to offer is time, care and space, companionship on a journey or on a small part of it. Be conscious that on this journey you are seeking to walk with another; and 'walking in step' at best is difficult; one is constantly tempted to rush ahead or to pull back or to

FROM DESPAIR TO HOPE

be distracted by what fascinates or seduces your attention, rather than concentrating your energies on being 'in step.' Most of the time you will not truly understand how the other feels. So don't say you do. You will not, must not, presume to provide them with answers or panaceas. It is very difficult to sit with the deep pain of another human without seeking to distract them or yourself from that pain or its effects.

It's so much easier to offer advice, or rush on to the next important task or appointment, or even to indulge in the distraction of making a cup of tea. That would be so much easier than staying with the survivor's feelings of overwhelming horror as they speak of their loved one's pain, the suffering of their last moments, the details of the death or finding the body. And yet it is through the telling and respectful hearing of such stories that moments of healing are discovered. Do not expect to be unaffected yourself by what you hear, and if you are someone whose work brings you often into such contacts, be careful to find for yourself the supports you need in order to fulfil your task. Every practising counsellor is expected to be in a relationship with another professional who acts as a guide and mentor, as well as offering support, comment and challenge around their work with others. Many who spend time listening find such a resource essential. Balance in your life and providing yourself with spaces in which you can reflect as well as spaces for enjoyment, creativity, excitement and distraction are also of great importance. Realise that no one can effectively listen to the pain of another for very long.

Here are some guidelines that it may be useful to observe, particularly if you find yourself becoming involved with more than one or two people who are in pain:

a) Prepare yourself; take time to reflect on the following questions. The answers may take some time to emerge. Why are you doing this anyway? Is it because you need confirmation of yourself as a caring person? Or because it is easier for you to relate to those who are vulnerable? Or because it comes as part of the package that is your job? Or is it because you sense, no matter how dimly, that you do have some feel for this situation? Come back often to these reflections.

Now – don't just rush in to be with the other; again prepare yourself. How are you feeling today? Is there anything going on for you that might distract you, or make it particularly difficult for you to be present, or to listen to certain areas today? If so, be realistic and either (i) decide to postpone your visit explaining why you are doing so to the other (it is far better to do this than to push ahead; your friend will pick up your blocks anyway. If however you can own them and explain what's going on for you they are far less likely to misinterpret what's happening or to feel rejected); *or* (ii) having recognised where you are at decide that you can put this aside until you have time later to deal with the issue(s) and go ahead with the conversation, perhaps explaining that you are a little sensitive around certain areas today.

Now consider the other person; how is s/he likely to be feeling, emotionally, physically, psychologically, spiritually and relationally? The focus of the question is not how you might feel in similar circumstances, but from what you know of the other, their context and their whole way of being to try to imagine or hypothesise how they might be in these areas of their life.

b) As you come to spend time with the other allow yourself not just to listen with your ears but also with your eyes and your intuition. (These will become more refined as you exercise them). What cues is the person offering as you move along? Listen to what people are saying and to what they are not saying. Notice the words they use and the speed of their sentences. Listen to their tone of voice, to their facial expression, to their body language – how they are sitting, standing, their facial colour and expression and so on. All these give clues as to whether the person is feeling upset, tense, frozen, fearful, and angry. Try to get some sense as to how the other person might find it useful to spend the time.

As the conversation unfolds the person will gradually reveal as much or as little as they wish to on this occasion. Respect this; don't rush them. They may have to test you little by little to see how you will deal with the information that they are sharing with to you. Remember they may have had some quite negative experiences from would-be listeners in the past. Remember too to periodically check as to whether you've understood what they've said correctly. This gives them an opportunity to correct you, to develop what they're saying if they wish to, or to reflect on it a little more themselves.

It's also important to check whether the person wishes to pursue a particular subject area at this time. Asking this explicitly gives them an opportunity to stop and think about this themselves or to change the subject if they wish to. It also and perhaps most importantly, conveys your concern for them.

Generally people are not asking you for answers; even if they are you probably do not have them. If you are asked such questions resist the temptation to play the professor; instead gently ask how they might answer the question themselves.

c) After spending time with someone who has been bereaved (and this goes for friends, relations and those whose work brings them into such contact, for instance youth leaders and clergy), consider the questions 'What was I trying to do there? What were my hidden expectations of myself?'(e.g. was I unrealistically expecting myself to cure pain?). As I honestly answer such questions, I may find that instead of seeking to accompany another, I seem to have been more occupied with trying to lead or push them, or indeed to protect myself from certain aspects of their (or my) experience. While this is a natural response, it may not have been helpful. As I begin to recognise such patterns in myself I can begin to be aware of them and to create change.

d) As a friend, relation or professional, recognise your limitations! Don't try to do what you cannot or what you are not equipped to. Remember there are also those specially trained to help who can offer support.

# YOUTH
# AND FAMILY ISSUES

## 7.1    Introduction

> Suicide is not a disease. It is an expression of a host
> of emotions; hopelessness, guilt, sorrow, loneliness,
> rage, fear, shame, that have their roots in
> psychological, social, medical, and biochemical
> factors
>
> (Psychological Society of Ireland, 1992)

It is a common practice to state why a person took their
own life, but in truth there is never just a single factor
behind a person's suicide but rather a range of
contributory factors that prevent someone coping with a
particular crisis or set of circumstances. Their 'coping'
mechanisms have broken down and suicide seems the only
way to cope.

In recent years there has been a dramatic increase in
death by suicide in the youth population especially among
young men. A report by UNICEF published in 1994

showed a rapid increase in suicide among young people over the previous two decades. The rate rose from 0.4 per 100,000 in 1970 to 7.5 per 100,000 in 1991. In 1997 in the Republic of Ireland a total of 111 young people took their own lives, 95 of which were male. Suicides in Britain among 15-24 year old males have risen from 58 per million in 1974 to 117 per million in 1990, an increase of 102 per cent. Hanging and suffocation were the main causes of death, followed by poisonous gases, particularly car exhaust fumes.

Trevor Lloyd, author of a report on suicide among young men, says that the causes of suicide are varied and complex. They range from mental illness, drug abuse and gender identity issues to child abuse, employment problems, homelessness, relationship troubles and physical illness or disability. An estimated 60 per cent of young men who take their own lives suffer from depression. Schizophrenia is also thought to be a major factor among this group.

Lloyd points out that men are less able than women to cope with change and much more reluctant to discuss personal problems. They also do not visit their doctor or call hospital help lines as often as women. Dr Ian Banks (Men's Health Forum) admitted that the 'lad culture' in Britain with its emphasis on drinking, fun and machismo could contribute to young men's inability to cope with their problems.

## 7.2    Contributory Factors

There are some contributory factors that may pre-dispose a young person to attempt suicide. These include:

*Changing family situation*
In both Northern Ireland and the Republic, society has changed rapidly in recent years with greater fragmentation and disintegration. The growth of nuclear

families has been rising rapidly as the extended family and rural networks have diminished. This has led to a decline in the numbers of young people who are linked into, and can access practical and emotional support from, wider family networks.

*Marital breakdown*
The growing incidence of marriage breakdown has a marked effect on the development and well-being of young people. In particular, the disruption and the discontinuity to the sense of stability, love, affection and care that are important to the development of self-esteem. The instability, guilt and confusion in the child or young person of separating parents is often linked to poor self-image and social skills amongst adolescents. These factors contribute to poor coping skills in managing stress in later life.

*Unemployment/poverty*
The links between suicide, unemployment and poverty are not clearly established. A loss of self-esteem, lack of purpose and an inability to contribute to society will have an effect on young people. It is thought that young men are particularly affected by job loss and extended unemployment.

*School pressures*
Young people are under increasing pressure because of growing demands in school. Parental expectations and increasing academic demands have an effect on students. A few well-publicised incidents point to bullying as a factor within suicides in the school population.

*Sexual identity*
Adolescence is a time of emerging sexual identity. This is not a smooth transition for many young people as they cope with enormous physical and emotional changes. This process can be a continual series of crises as teenagers

grow into maturity. There are a variety of views about the relationship between gay and lesbian sexuality and youth suicide. If it is difficult for the heterosexual young person then it is clearly much more difficult for those whose orientation is gay or lesbian. They may face alienation within society, harassment, homophobic reaction and loss of family support. This can place huge stresses on young people at a time of great vulnerability.

### Changing cultural and religious practices
Attitudes to religion have changed radically in the past decade and young people have witnessed a loss of confidence in the institutions of religious faith. 'Traditional Christian values and practices offered many things. Amongst them was an attempt to give an explanation and philosophy to live without ignoring pain which is never far from human existence...'. (M.J.Kelleher)

### Alcohol and drug abuse
Growing familiarity and abuse of alcohol and drugs has led to addictive behaviours among young people. Alcohol and drug abuse is very prevalent in this age range and is a very significant factor in youth suicide.

### Suicides glamorised in youth culture
Some of the pop icons of youth culture have committed suicide and a few performers have glamorised it. The lyrics of some of the songs have introduced the idea that suicide is an option. In some cases parents and educators have blamed such lyrics for having a very negative effect on vulnerable young people.

### Increased availability of methods of suicide
Access to methods of suicide has a noticeable bearing on suicide rates. Car exhaust poisoning is one of the most frequent methods employed by young men. Does the

increased ownership of cars coupled with publicity about such deaths explain some of the increase in the suicide rate among young men?

## 7.3    The Role of the Youth Worker

Youth workers can make a very significant and important contribution to the well-being of the young people with whom they work. They should be alert to young people who:

- Have made a previous suicide attempt
- Talk of suicide or making a plan
- Have a strong wish to die, preoccupation with death or are giving away prized possessions
- Have signs of depression, such as moodiness, hopelessness or withdrawal
- Have increased alcohol and/or drug use
- Have a friend/family member who has recently committed suicide
- Show impulsiveness and are taking unnecessary risks; or
- Lack connection to family and friends (no one to talk to)

How can you help?

*Suicidal behaviour is a cry for help*
'If someone is going to end their life nothing can stop them'. The suicidal person is ambivalent – partly they want to live and partly they want the pain to end. If a person turns to you they are doing a positive thing and believe you are trustworthy and can help them. Be willing to give and get help sooner rather than later.

Unfortunately suicidal people are often afraid that in trying to get help their pain will be intensified. They fear that they will be told they are stupid, foolish, sinful or manipulative; or will face rejection, punishment, suspension from school or written records of their condition. Everything must be done to reduce pain rather than increase or prolong it.

### Active listening

Give the person every opportunity to unburden themselves and ventilate their feelings. You don't need to say much and there are no magic words. Offer patience, empathy and acceptance, and avoid arguments or giving advice.

Ask 'Are you having thoughts of suicide?' If the subject is brought up you may in fact be giving the person an opening to talk about something they have not dared broach with anyone else. This provides a further opportunity to discharge pent-up and painful feelings. A large number of people do have suicidal feelings and are relieved to talk about them.

If they are acutely suicidal do not leave them alone. Someone who is 'on the edge' needs constant care – try and get help as quickly as possible. Don't leave them on their own.

Urge professional help. Don't think that a few friendly chats will help sort out the problems of a suicidal person. In any referral situation let the person know that you are still available to them and want to maintain contact and support.

### No secrets

The young person may want to keep your conversation strictly confidential – do not promise that. You will need advice on how to accompany the person as they move through this traumatic experience. Parents must be informed of such feelings as they are ultimately responsible for the care of the young person.

### From crisis to recovery

Most people have suicidal thoughts or feelings at some point in their lives, yet less than 2 per cent of all deaths result from suicide. Your task is to support the person as they build coping strategies.

*Helping the group after a member's suicide*
How can a youth worker help their group after a member's suicide? The leaders of the group will need to give thought to the following:

- How and when should the other group members be informed?
- What should be done about the victim's close friends?
- Are there other high risk members?
- Should there be a symbolic expression of grief?
- What arrangements should be made for the group's attendance at the funeral?
- Would a visit to the victim's parents be helpful?
- Are there appropriate commemorative activities the group should engage in?

What any young person contemplating suicide needs most is a trusted friend who will listen, accept and help them reflect on the consequences of their actions. The message the young person needs to get is that they have a friend who will walk with them through their darkest moments and that they are loved and cherished by that person, their family and their friends.

## 7.4   The Suicide of Young People and its Impact on the Family

Suicide is a word that at one time was seldom mentioned in conversation. Nowadays, we hear the word suicide used in an apparently casual way in every day conversation, in rap music and pop songs. 'If I looked like that I'd commit suicide'; 'I feel like committing suicide.' Sir Ronnie Flanagan, then Chief Constable of the Police Service of

Northern Ireland, in response to criticisms made by the Police Ombudsman relating to the Omagh bomb incident, was reported as saying that he would commit suicide in public if he believed that the criticisms were true.

The word is often used in a casual way, yet at the same time the incidence of suicide among young people is extraordinarily and frighteningly high. Suicide may be seen as a statement or a symbol of the acute distress of the deceased and in turn the experience of a death by suicide of a young person in the family leaves the families in acute pain and sorrow, never to return to their previous state.

For many families the greatest difficulty they experience is trying to make sense of why a young person could choose to die, rather than talk with their families and seek out the love and support that they needed. Many are drawn to the literature to try to learn more about suicide, to see if within all this information there is a glimmer of an explanation. Helpers, officials and personnel involved at the time of the death will be drawn into this process of searching for explanations with family members.

Suicide is known throughout history and is romanticised in period dramas such as *Romeo and Juliet* and in modern movies such as *Crouching Tiger Hidden Dragon*. For both Church and State the act of suicide has presented a real moral challenge – can suicide be condoned? Historically both the Church of England and the Catholic Church denied a burial service/funeral rites to those who died by suicide, while Jewish custom was concerned that no honour was bestowed on those who died by their own hand. In Islamic tradition suicide is a very grave crime and it is also a source of great shame in Hindu faith. Suicide was a criminal offence in England and Wales until 1961 and in Ireland until 1993, unlike Scotland where suicide was not regarded as a criminal offence.

Choosing one's own death is historically associated with offending God, laying one's soul vulnerable to evil influence, and being a criminal. While the law and the churches have relaxed their punitive approach to suicide much of the ethos of moral disapproval remains in communities (including religious communities) and cultures. The overtones of shame continue to prevail and set the scene for grieving families, creating a barrier of embarrassment and shame between them and the friends and neighbours who could offer the support they need most. This shame influences officials and community members, as well as family members and is a factor in the belief that suicide statistics are way below the actual incidence. Coroners and police officers may believe that they are being kind to the family by suggesting that the evidence points to a death by misadventure rather than one by suicide. This may even be the case in a suicide by hanging or gunshot, especially if there is no suicide note, as is often the case. Under-reporting is likely for all instances of suicide but is thought to be most common in the cases of children and adolescents. Perhaps officials are considering issues such as life insurance as well as concrete evidence and people's sensitivities (and, of course, strictly speaking suicide is never the cause of death, rather the nature of it), but for many families who are convinced that the death was one of suicide a confirmation, if possible, would be affirming and welcome. However, the inquest usually follows many months of searching and seeking explanations and for families is a necessary, if painful, return to the details of the death, hoping for more information and for an affirmation of the outcome of their own search.

There can be few experiences in life that are as painful, as all pervasive and as enduring as when a son or daughter dies after taking their own life. Yet each year, for thousands of families in the Western world this is their reality. In England and Wales, the rates of people aged 15-24 years of age taking their own life in 1997 was 16.4 per hundred thousand. In the Republic of Ireland for 1998 it was 13.6 per hundred thousand, and in the North of Ireland 7.4 per hundred thousand. Scotland has the highest death rate for young people, with 600 young people dying as a result of suicide in 1998, as compared to 28 in Northern Ireland. One year on, in Northern Ireland, the number of deaths of young people had increased by eight, to 36. These rates refer to deaths deemed to be as a result of suicide determined by Coroners' Courts. Such is the nature of evidence required by these Courts before coming to such a decision that many experts in this field think that the true numbers can be up to twice as many as the official figures suggest. Young men take their own lives at a rate four times higher than young women in UK, and eleven times higher in Ireland.

Possibly as many as 80 per cent of the deaths of young people, can be understood as part of a mental health condition – usually of depression, manic depression or schizophrenia. Schizophrenia commonly onsets in the late teens or early twenties, particularly in young men, and is associated with an increased risk of suicide by as much as fifteen times that of the population generally. Sadly, even with psychiatric help, both within and outside hospital, the risk of suicide remains high.

Depression can be overlooked as a feature of life for substantial numbers of adolescents and youth. Some parents reflect after the death that, with hindsight, they were unable to recognise signs of depression in their son or daughter as the person was usually quiet or because they thought that moodiness was to be expected in adolescence. Even where depression has been recognised and treatment begun, families may falsely have thought that the risk of suicide had passed, noticing that they seemed calmer. This apparent improvement in their mental state could reflect an inner calm stemming from a decision having been taken to end their life. Very often it is as people are making a recovery from depression that the risk of suicide becomes most serious. This may be explained as having new strength and energy to act upon suicidal feelings. Bereavement in the family increases the risk of suicide, just as the suicide itself leads to more bereavement, depression and further risk of suicide of a family member.

Schizophrenia can also be overlooked by families. In the early stages of the illness as the young person experiences bizarre thoughts or visions, they may be aware that others will be alarmed by what is happening to them. Perhaps their first attempts at trying to explain their experiences with a contemporary were received by shock or a negative reaction. If the thoughts are suicidal they may be kept well away from close family members. Frequent contact does not necessarily let us see the other person's inner world.

The increased use of alcohol and drugs amongst young people can certainly exacerbate or even trigger a deteriorating mental condition. In the modern family young people often live relatively separate lives in their own rooms, using a personal computer or video, making it more difficult for families to be aware of mood changes, agitation, or personal concerns.

For the remaining 20 per cent who take their own lives, there are numerous reasons for this: pressure of work; feelings of not being able to cope; seeking to avoid a painful or embarrassing event; guilt, shame, anger; wanting to hurt somebody; feeling unloved or worthless; acting in a fit of pique – all can play a part. Some have been abused sexually or physically, some have worries about a health condition, or their developing sexuality, while others feel trapped by a conflict within their culture. The young person in solitary confinement prison, or the teenager exposed to merciless bullying at school, may experience their immediate circumstances as intolerable. For others, their decision can seem hasty and based upon very little substance. What is most significant is that what may seem like a relatively minor or resolvable problem can be intolerable for a young person with low self-esteem and little hope for the future. Rural and urban families are at risk, as are all classes, but it is the working class and the unemployed who are most at risk of a death by suicide among the young men in their family. The young person who dies from suicide is frequently very talented and artistic and creative, so the sense of hopelessness is based on feelings and emotions rather than ability or performance.

Some families say that they can't think of anything that their lost son or daughter couldn't have shared with them and this is undoubtedly true. Others have known of their son's intolerable pain and wish for death and have tried by all means to seek help. The knowledge that they have failed to convince a health professional of the severity of the risk and the need for in-patient treatment haunts many families.

But it is often another young person who catches a glimpse of their friend's inner world of thoughts of death and escape, or of delusions and thoughts of sacrifice. Young people need to become aware of the risk of suicide among their friends and classmates and to be aware of the network of help available. Finding help for a friend through youth workers or pastors, through health workers or counsellors or by contacting their parents is not a betrayal of confidence, it is a necessary life line. The knowledge that someone has suicidal thoughts needs to be shared, not kept as a confidence.

Although men are more likely to die as a result of suicide, women generally are two or three times more likely to *attempt* suicide or self harm than men. This may be partly explained by the fact that women are more likely to take an overdose of tablets while men more commonly carry out suicide by hanging, jumping from a height, by cutting themselves or by gunshot. There is a complex relationship between self-harm/attempted suicide and successful suicide. Some people repeatedly self-harm by cutting themselves or overdosing, inclining us to take their actions less seriously, or at least to view self harm and attempted suicide as a very different phenomenon from suicide. What is more likely is that there is a continuum connecting self-harming behaviour and attempted and successful suicides. If we are fortunate enough to be aware of a cry for help in the form of self-harm/attempted suicide it is important to respond in a way that can help to relieve the pain and distress, since it is known that a suicide attempt is an important indicator of someone at risk of taking their own life in the future.

While the shock of the death and the attempt to explain it may rip a family apart, the bereavement also has the potential to bind the remaining members together, at least in the first instance. However, as different family members deal with the bereavement in their own way and at their own pace, even the bereavement response has the potential to be divisive.

Twelve families in Britain and Northern Ireland, during 2001-2002, took part in lengthy video interviews sharing their experiences of the death of a young person in their family. These interviews are edited to about twenty-five or thirty minutes each and form part of a training pack for people working with bereaved families and in suicide prevention (see Resources – Appendix A). These contribute to some of the insights shared in this chapter.

Some of the young men who died had shared their recurring wish to die with their family and had been referred for psychiatric help. Three had received in-patient treatment, although in each of these instances their families felt that the help came late, had to be fought for, and that they were discharged as not being at risk of suicide when this seemed blatantly not to be the case. Another young man had phoned his family a few hours before his death to tell them he loved them. They had been worried about his changed behaviour and thought this was due to drugs and alcohol. But for most the death came unpredicted and unexpected, although some of the young people were having difficulties at school, with relationships, or were in a Young Offenders' Centre in isolation, for example. One young man who died in isolation could not bear to be alone, even when in his own home.

Whether the death was totally unpredicted or whether for long there had been the feeling that it would happen one day; the death itself invariably comes as a great shock. Feelings of disbelief are almost universal with the conviction that there has been some terrible mistake being reluctantly surrendered only when the body has been seen. The acknowledgement is often accompanied by numbness, by a freezing of emotions and by an appearance of coping but in a world that is feeling very unreal – like acting or going through the motions, but not quite belonging to or being part of what is happening. Responses are essentially unique to the individual and while many remain zombie-like and dry-eyed some may cry almost hysterically for long periods of time, while others go about the business seemingly totally unaffected by their loss, only to suffer breakdown some months later. For the group who took part in this video training pack it seemed that fathers were more likely to become physically ill and to be incapacitated for days, weeks or even months while mothers seem to be depressed and distressed over longer periods of time.

The family usually has to contend with the police investigation amidst the shock and horror of the death. The police, in turn, often have to tell family members what has happened and have to investigate the circumstances of the death and gather evidence for the inquest. Some families found that their home became invaded by police searching for evidence, while the family were isolated in a room. Loved ones invariably want to hug and talk to their dead child or brother or sister; to sit with them and hold their hand. One family could only visit their son after he was taken to the police mortuary, and even then could only see him through glass. This contrasts with others who felt tremendous sensitivity and support from the officials at their home. At this very sensitive time little things become very important – handling possessions and giving them to the family (not just setting them aside where they can be found).

At the time of the funeral, perhaps just a few days, or at most a week or two following death, the majority are likely to still be in a very dazed state and will be able to recall little of the actual event, some family members may be too distressed to attend while others are able to plan the service and take an active part in it. Yet the funeral is a very significant event as an opportunity to honour the young person and to acknowledge their love for them. Yet, despite all the organisation and detailed planning the funeral often passes as a cloud or haze of confusion, not least for the young people in the family.

The grave can be a source of comfort and place to focus one's grief. Some family members, especially mothers, feel they need to visit the grave daily. The family may feel the need to stay with their dead son physically and be reluctant to move to another town or region.

Bereavement happens at a different pace for family members and grief is expressed in different ways. While the whole family is changed forever they may not always be able to 'be there for each other' all of the time. Some young people felt they could not burden their parents with their own sorrow and distress, as they were already in such great sorrow and distress from the suicide. Young people relied on partners, if they were in relationships, for support, while others were trying to cope alone. Teenage friends, especially young men, do not seem to have the capacity to understand or support a young person in distress and the young person remains essentially alone with their problem. How hard it is for a young person who is meeting new people and making new friends to respond to the question, 'Do you have any brothers or sisters?', to cope with the guilt of what has been said before the death, to experience the sense of abandonment, to understand and forgive. These young people had managed to forgive and even to some extent to understand, but they more than the older parents, felt passionately and intensely angry that their brother could decide to do this. The death also put their own life on hold at a critical time of study or in the early years of work. One teenage girl felt she became the sister of the boy who hanged himself, rather than being herself. Another young man was unable to proceed with his college life and his life became unfocussed and troubled, taking drugs, getting into debt, relationships failing.

As with all bereavements, but possibly more poignantly, there are significant hurdles after the death – meeting friends and neighbours, returning to work, birthdays and anniversaries and Christmas. Most people seem to experience the awkwardness of others after a suicide in the family. The avoidance of the pain or having to cope with the upset of close family is stark, as people leave the shop without completing their shopping or cross the road to avoid an encounter in the street. Returning to work, colleagues try to talk about other things – everything but the most painful and significant thing that is in the forefront of everyone's mind. These are symbols of discomfort that indicate to families that they should not discuss their pain or be upset. Mentioning the death does not add to the pain and upset, it just brings it into the open.

One mother interviewed, Anita Oxtoby, whose 16-year old son took his own life, expressed this point very well:

> I would like to say that if people see someone who has been bereaved it is important to acknowledge the bereavement and not to shy away from the fact that someone very important to them has died. If it

is awkward for them or they do not know what to say, they should simply say that they were very sorry to hear that ____ had died. It hurts an awful lot to learn that that person knows about a death but doesn't say anything and that the dead person is forgotten or not mentioned because they find it awkward. They don't have to mention it every time but certainly the first time a bereaved person is seen after the death, its very important to say it then. It will help them; even if at the mention of the name they cry. The hurt is an ongoing hurt – the hurt is every day of every week for a long time and mentioning the dead person's name is not going to cause them hurt. They might be momentarily upset but it won't be long before they recover themselves. The hurt of not mentioning the dead person lasts much longer.

The first Christmas without a young family member is hard to bear and a number of families choose to be away from home. Like the inquest, birthdays and the anniversary of the death are very difficult, as are events in which the young person would have been involved, such as school exam results, graduation and such like.

### The Christian response
Restricting the burial of those who had died by their own hand to unconsecrated areas of churchyards was but one example of humans seeking to exercise the wrath of God when He has bidden us to show forth his love. It was an example taken in ignorance of the last moments of a human life and regardless of whether or not there was the confession of an anguished soul and the forgiveness of a loving Father. The location of the grave of a loved family member in a particular section of a burial ground was a perpetual reminder of his sin and society's and the churches' attitude toward it. The attitude also to the

family of which he was a part. For those that are left the pain of loss and grief is added to by the hurt of criticism and rejection.

While burial restrictions are no more, many of the myths surrounding suicide and ideas about the family circumstances in which those taking their own lives were born and raised remain with us. For the 20 per cent of young people taking their own lives where there is no indication of mental illness, research has failed to find any significant associating factor that is not also associated with the more than 99 per cent of young people who to not take their own lives. So families associated with a young person's suicide and families not so associated are not in other ways significantly different. In many ways we wish that it were not so. It would be comforting and reassuring to know that ours is not the sort of family that give rise to a young person's suicide; that we lack those factors (whatever they might be) that create such tragedies. Condemning families that experience such an event help us to feel different and therefore safe. But we are not different, thus have no justification for criticism or rejection and no grounds whatsoever for feeling safe.

No family has any built-in immunity, we are all at risk. At risk of the spontaneous adolescent gesture, the fit of anger, hurt, shame, embarrassment or fear; and from the consequences – likely to last in some form as long as life itself. The death of a young person by suicide is not merely a family matter, it is the concern of the neighbourhood, the community and, particularly, the Church.

How then ought Christians to respond to such a tragedy? In broadest terms, to bear one another's burdens and to show forth the love of God. Many Christians want to do this but do not know how and do not want to intrude. They end up by doing nothing. Almost every grieving family member wants to be stopped in the street or visited at home and to hear the words, 'I am so very sorry to hear about...'. They want to hear especially from those that they know, but also from others. It gives the assurance that they are not being condemned for having let this happen, not being marginalised and that they are still part of the human race, however frozen of dazed they may be feeling. Condolence cards are good but no substitute for a letter and neither is a satisfactory substitute for a face-to-face contact. Resist the platitudes (he's gone to a better place, all the pain is over now or whatever) and do not place the dead person on a pedestal and say nice things about him that were not true. There are no words that can lift the grieving person up from their sadness so do not try to find them, thereby giving them the added burden of pretending that your words are a great comfort to them when they are not. If they want to say these things that's all right – don't argue about them. Just being alongside, staying a while, listening if they want to talk but not initiating anything yourself is probably the best thing. Except for one thing!

Ask how you can help. For a few weeks, families are likely to be in a state of shock and do not cope very well. There may be practical things that need attention like shopping, driving, cooking and providing meals. There are ideal opportunities for a church team here. Visits from friends and neighbours usually lessen dramatically soon after the funeral. The need for them does not although the need for practical help generally diminishes after two or three weeks. With the loss of a child through suicide, two to three years is not an excessive time for feeling both low and vulnerable and appreciative of regular visits from caring people. It is important not to exploit the vulnerability of grieving families through taking over aspects of their lives, however kindly intended. It is essential that they are involved and remain the decision takers in all matters. Grief is not a good time for taking big decisions so do not raise big issues that require an answer unless there really are very urgent ones. Your involvement should contribute to the creation of a quiet, peaceful atmosphere.

As a Christian, you will want to pray for the grieving family both on your own and with others from your Fellowship. Should you pray with the grieving family? They may well be feeling very angry with God for taking a loved one and project this anger on to you for even suggesting it. Understand what an angry outburst means and do not be put off from helping by this. If it seems right and you gently or tentatively suggest that you might pray with them at some stage, if they agree, ask what they would like prayer to be for. Likely ones are that their loved one is with the Lord, that no other member of the family will take his/her own life, that they will be helped to cope with the deep pain that they are experiencing, that God's protection and peace will be upon them and that they will experience God's presence and closeness to them.

There are some significant differences between a suicide of a young person and deaths through other reasons. For many surviving relatives the feelings of vulnerability, rejection, hurt, anger and questioning never quite go away; not even after many years. Church prayer groups need to remember them and uphold them.

FROM DESPAIR TO HOPE

# PART III

# RESPONDING AS CHURCHES

*This third section builds on the earlier sections to consider how the organised Church can respond in dealing with circumstances of suicide within its community*

8. The Role of the Church

9. Worship

# THE ROLE OF THE CHURCH

## 8.1    The Church

'The Church' can mean different concepts to different people. To some the Church is the building at the crossroads, which is part of a chain. It represents an institution with its structures, administrative systems, and culture.

For others the Church is the body of people, linked together by a common faith in Christ, each member having a responsibility towards the other, and seeking to live out the implications of that shared faith in today's world.

The former could be likened to the shell of the mollusc, attached to a rock on the seashore – the latter to the living organism inside, with all its capacity for movement in response to its environment and for creating new life.

It is this latter identity that is being mainly thought of as we consider the role of the Church in relation to suicide.

When Jesus was preparing to leave his disciples, he took them away and gave them their commission (Matt

28:18-19) – 'All authority in heaven and on earth has been given to me, therefore go and make disciples of all nations'. This pattern of ministry was set by our Lord for the Church, to bring people to an understanding of and faith in their heavenly father. This involves being open to people, in all their varied circumstances, and meeting them at their point of 'need' – the sick, the distraught, the marginalised, the embezzler, the adulterer, the rich, and those who thought they were 'fine', and were experts in religious matters.

To live out the compassion of Christ for people in need is as much part of the calling of the Church as is teaching and preaching.

## 8.2    Suicide

Suicide is defined as the successful attempt to kill oneself.

The method of suicide attempt varies from relatively non-violent actions such as poisoning, overdose, and inhaling car exhaust, to violent methods such as shooting, hanging or cutting oneself.

The person who has come to the point of suicide has reached the place of despair. Among the feelings that have been identified are: isolation, restlessness, loneliness, and the lack of a philosophy of life that can bring comfort.

More than 90 per cent of all suicides are related to emotional or psychiatric illness. When these distresses are placed alongside grief, shock, stigma, taboo, guilt and anger – the range of feelings and attitudes with which the bereaved by suicide have to cope – it makes for a truly traumatic scenario.

Within the Church there can be additional pain, linked to questions within people's minds about 'taking life' and eternal destiny. There can also be the misguided idea that Christians shouldn't suffer from depression – which may have been what triggered the suicide – and this can add an additional burden of shame.

## 8.3    The Church's Role

In the midst of such suffering, the Church must ask –
'What would Jesus want it to say about all of this?'

Surely the Church's role is to act in ways that
demonstrate the compassion of a God who cares for each
individual to the extent of incarnation and crucifixion.
That is some challenge! Where can the Church start?

*Belief into practice*
The regular coming together in worship, affirming the
sovereignty of God in our individual and collective life and
listening to Him, is the shared activity within the
structure of the institutional Church, where people find
strength and grace to put belief into practice.

*Openness*
If the Church is an obedient community, it will be open to
the individual needs of people, and aware of the
importance of affirmation, which builds healthy self-
esteem. It will identify the potential contribution that its
members can make to the practical and spiritual life of the
church. A by-product of this is a sense of worth and
belonging.

The difficulties that people encounter in life should be
the subject of the Church's pastoral care, which is in some
ways a collective responsibility. The bearing of one
another's burdens, and caring for those in need, is meant
to be part of the ongoing life of the Church.

This openness to people's needs begins within the
Church, but is meant to be inherent in its outreach to
God's world.

*Listening*
A genuine care for another involves providing a listening
ear. Such listening means not only taking time for one's
neighbour, but listening in depth to him or her and being

alert to the emotions beneath the words – the fears, disappointments, hopes and dreams. This action can be comforting and strengthening, as each person is shown that they matter, they are understood and are not 'alone'.

If the Church learns to be open, to care and to listen, then it can help withstand the negative movement towards fragmentation and individualism that is present in our society. The Church would thereby be contributing to health and healing, and countering some of the forces that can sweep people further down the road of quiet desperation.

*Acceptance*

Acceptance of people means showing them respect for their unique identity. The Church should provide a haven to which people feel they can come – just as they are – without fear of condemnation or a judgmental attitude. After all, the Church is made up of sinners who have weaknesses and shortcomings. 'There is none perfect!' The only difference from those outside is that Church members believe in a God to whom they can come for forgiveness, and they are charged to extend the same mercy and forgiveness to others that they receive from God.

There is a temptation to keep up appearances in the Church, acting as though there were no personal difficulties. This is not helpful. The Church should be a community where there is humility and realism about the struggles in life. This can reduce internal stress and enable people to share honestly and so strengthen one another.

One test of acceptance is how people respond to suicide.

People within the Church can display the same reactions as those in society generally, for example, blaming, denial or distancing from the reality of what has happened. This is linked to misunderstanding and ignorance.

It was only in 1993 that suicide was decriminalised in Ireland, and even more recently that understanding about its causes has grown. It is now acknowledged that at least 90 per cent of people who die by suicide have diminished responsibility.

Sadly, uninformed responses can deny the compassion of Christ for those caught up in the aftermath of a suicide, which affects a lot of people. It is estimated that in Ireland a minimum of fifty people suffer as a result of a single suicide.

*Support and understanding*
When the tragedy of suicide implodes in a circle of family, friends and acquaintances, help and support is needed. Those bereaved are dealing with much more than shock and grief. They have the cocktail of guilt, blame, shame, anger, and so on, as well as coping with the reactions of other people.

It is important that those who are bereaved know that others are aware of their anguish. This can be expressed through sending a card, by a visit or a telephone call, as well as by assurance of prayer on their behalf. Actions such as hospitality, sensitively offered, or gifts of flowers or food such as a home-made pie, can also convey love and support. Being mindful of the anniversary of the death, as would apply to other deaths, also shows thoughtfulness and care.

## 8.4    Unhelpful Reactions

*Isolation*
As already mentioned, suicide has taboo and stigma attached to it. This can lead to a conspiracy of silence surrounding the event, leaving the bereaved with a sense of aloneness that adds to the pain.
The Church community should ensure that this does not happen. Leaders and members need to be informed about how suicide can affect those left behind, in order to respond appropriately and with sensitivity.

It is healing to be given the opportunity to speak about those things that weigh heavily on the heart. The distress of suicide needs to be shared.

## Denial

Denial can be defined as unwillingness to accept reality. This is because the reality is too disturbing or painful. An example of denial is when a person refuses acceptance of a diagnosis about the terminal nature of an illness.

Suicide is highly disturbing. The fact that someone has felt so desperate that they have taken steps to terminate what others strive to sustain is hard to handle. There can be an emotional block to acknowledging the prevalence and the predisposing factors to suicide.

Within the Church community, an added factor in denial can be the difficulty in accepting that a Christian could feel so hard pressed with what has being going on in their lives that they become submerged by it all – 'Christians should not be depressed'. This can be seen as denial of the faith. But Christians do become exhausted and ill. Failure to accept this can result in danger signals not being picked up, and necessary action not being taken to provide help for the person who is suffering.

## Suppression of anger

When someone about whom we care dies it is not unknown to experience feelings of anger during the process of grieving. In the case of suicide, the probability of anger being present is greater. Relatives and friends may feel it could have been prevented. If the person who has died has been receiving medical help, anger may be directed towards doctors or the hospital. Relatives may blame each other for not picking up warning signals. A difficult work environment or a strained relationship may be the focus of angry feelings.

Anger can also be felt against the person who has taken their own life. 'Why did they do this to me? It was selfish of them to leave me to cope with all these problems.' It may be that the tenor of the suicide note portrays aggression and this then adds to feelings of anger.

There are some who find the expression of anger difficult to handle, and try to stem it. In Church circles there can be the added discomfort of those who think displaying anger is 'wrong'. This has no biblical foundation. Anger is part of our repertoire of emotions as human beings, and it can be a healthy response to hurt and injustice. Bottled up anger is harmful to people. It can affect health or be displaced on to other issues, which can cause other complications. A healthy Church community will allow anger to be expressed.

*Unrelieved guilt feelings*
When suicide occurs it is very common for the bereaved to have strong feelings of guilt. There can be a lurking feeling of being in some way responsible for what has happened, that warning signs should have been recognised and help sought.

Feelings of guilt need to be talked through, and not pushed away and allowed to fester. Sometimes relatives and friends can have a false sense of guilt. This should be identified as such. It needs to be affirmed that no one can take the responsibility for keeping another person alive, when they want to end their life.

If the feelings of guilt have any foundation, one of the key messages of the Christian faith is that of forgiveness when wrong is acknowledged.

## 8.5    The Church and Social Action

In this section the concept of Church could be taken to mean the institutional structure, which can act in a representative capacity. As such the Church has a role in speaking and acting as a collective influence, tackling issues in communities and society that need to be addressed.

The following is an example of such action:

In 1997 in Ballynahinch, County Down, there was a spate of suicides among young men aged seventeen to twenty-five years. None had Church connections. Concern among the churches in the town led to a coming together to confer and then to act. They felt that there was a need to do something about building relationships, that there should be a place where young people could come together, which would not be identified with church property. The aim was to provide an environment where young people could drop in and relax, where friendships could be nourished, and a sense of community could be fostered, where individuals could feel valued. It was to be an antidote to aloneness.

Grants were sought, a base was acquired and equipment purchased. 'A bar with no beer' was part of the facility. The project was named 'The Edge' and its mission statement as 'empowering young people to discover new perspectives in life.' Six youth leaders were provided by the main churches in the town. Volunteers were also recruited.

The outcome to date? Individuals, who would normally have fought each other if they were to meet outside, are relaxed in each other's company. Relationships have been strengthened. New ones are being formed. Good relationships between young people and leaders have been established. The Edge is frequented by both Protestants and Roman Catholics.

It is the vision of the leaders that the experiences in The Edge will take young people away from the edge, where there is fear, darkness and hopelessness, and where young people will come to know the love of God. This is one example of an initiative by the churches, when faced with malaise in their area.

## 8.6    In Summary

There needs to be a growth in awareness about the realities surrounding suicide. As the prevalence of suicide has been increasing in Ireland, so the churches should become better informed about risk factors, and what can be done to help.

The sensitive care of those who have been bereaved by suicide must be a particular concern of the Church community. Where there is anxiety about the spiritual destiny of the deceased the compassion of God should be demonstrated by His Church for those whose minds are disturbed.

The Church should strive to model healthy, caring environments, where people know that they matter. Individual members may feel prompted to serve in helping organisations such as the Samaritans and Cruse Bereavement care.

Initiatives to combat unhealthy trends in society should be intrinsic in the life and acre of the church.

# RITUAL AND WORSHIP

In this chapter, we consider the importance of using ritual in the context of suicide, as an important resource that contributes to healing. Worship is part of the richness that ritual offers. In the later part of this chapter, we look at some possible examples and structures for use in such worship contexts.

## 9.1    Introduction to Using Worship

In a situation where a family is traumatised by the loss of someone as a result of suicide, there may be an initial desire to conceal the nature of the death that has occurred. In view of this, it is necessary for a pastoral minister to work with the family in helping them to accept the reality of the situation and to be open to the support of friends and the Christian community in their bereavement. Only then can the family be introduced to the idea that worship has an important role in helping them to respond to God's loving care for them.

How can one use the word 'worship' when addressing a situation as tragic as that of suicide? Only, I think, if one understands it as a concept that can contain our prayer, our anguish, our anger and desperation, and our hope.

I remember when two distant cousins of mine, who were brothers in their late teens, fell in love with the same girl. It ended tragically when the younger brother threw himself in the river and drowned. That is the closest encounter I have had among my family and friends, but it was enough to give me some inkling of the shock and disbelief that people feel when someone close to them feels that life is no longer worth living and takes their own life.

For those of us with pastoral responsibilities, or those concerned for families coping with this trauma, we need to bear in mind that as well as the grief of bereavement, they are probably feeling shocked and bewildered. They may also be have feelings of guilt that they should have done more to prevent it happening.

For a pastor or well-meaning friend to provide facile answers and reassurances may not help at this stage. Our worship, used in the broad sense of the word, must be grounded in reality and echo the God who became incarnate and shares in all our human experiences, our sorrows as well as our joys.

## 9.2    Using the Psalms and Similar Scripture

The first and the most heart-felt prayer of those who loved the deceased is probably, 'Oh God – why?' and 'Where were you, God, when this happened? Couldn't you have saved him/her?'

If those ministering to them show shock or concern that the bereaved are questioning God like this, then it can compound the sense of guilt that may be part of the reaction to a suicide by the family or friends. Instead, it may be appropriate to use suitable psalms expressing a similar sense of anguish or even anger towards God in order to reassure people that this is recognised as part of our genuine communication with God.

The psalms are also useful because some show a glimmer of light at the end of the tunnel as they often conclude with an expression of trust in God in spite of all that has happened.

The circumstances of the suicide will also have a bearing upon how one approaches those who are bereaved and one's choice of psalms or similar parts of Scripture. The sudden and violent death of a young person evokes very different reactions among relatives and friends from those experienced when someone who has suffered a long and painful illness ends her/his life in desperation. In the latter case, the bereaved may be helped by the reassurance that God's love and understanding is infinitely greater than our own.

## 9.3    Using Simple Prayer Formats

Because the atmosphere in the home or among the bereaved may be highly emotional, it can be helpful to have a simple structured form of prayer that involves the bereaved but only invites short responses.

The brief formats offered here are only examples and may be used separately or combined into a longer one. They should be amended to suit the particular situation and the specific faith context of the bereaved. Some families may be very unfamiliar with the Christian idiom whilst others may have strong connections with a Church community.

*Sample formats*

(A) *Prayers Seeking Comfort in Distress*

| | |
|---|---|
| Opening sentences: | 2 Corinthians 1:3 and 4. |
| Leader: | Jesus cried out from the cross, 'My God, my God, why have you forsaken me?' |
| | In our pain and desolation, we too can feel abandoned by God and so we ask ... |
| All: | Lord, have mercy. |
| Leader: | The prophet Jeremiah cried out to God that his enemies had dug a pit to bury him and threatened his life. |
| | When doubt and anxiety threaten to engulf us, we pray ... |
| All: | Christ, have mercy |
| Leader: | God assures us that he will never fail us or forsake us. In darkness, in emptiness and in confusion, we are not alone. |
| All: | Lord, have mercy. |
| Leader: | Let us pray. |
| | Creator God, we are your children who come from you and return to you; you are our home and our source of comfort and strength. In our grief and distress, not knowing where to turn, we take refuge in your embracing love. |
| | We pray for all gathered here, and all who are thinking about us at this time: give us courage to hold on, release from despair and feelings of guilt, and a |

foothold upon the rock of your fidelity to us when the mists of doubt and hopelessness swirl around us.

We commit _____ into your strong and gentle love and safekeeping; may your light draw him/her through the shadow of death and into the peace of your presence.

We remember your promise that you will complete in each one of us the work you have begun, whether our earthly life is long or short, so we pray that we may all know completeness in your kingdom where we shall rejoice together.

We make our prayer through Christ our Life-giver.

Amen.

## (B) *Prayers Remembering the One Who Has Died*

| | |
|---|---|
| Symbolic action: | The lighting of a candle. |
| Leader: | Nothing happens on earth without God knowing it. If God knows about the sparrow that falls to the ground, how much more is God's concern when the flame of life has gone from our sight. |
| Symbolic action | The lighted candle is shielded to hide the flame but to allow the light to be seen around the edges of the shield. |
| Leader: | By remembering _____ we allow our memories to enable us to see the light of his/her life that is still present with us although we cannot see the flame from which it emanates. |

|  |  |
|---|---|
|  | So we pray, In the darkness of our pain and loneliness, |
| All: | God be with us. |
| Leader: | We remember \_\_\_\_\_'s journey from the safety of the womb into the complexity of the world, we recall that pain delivered the joy of a child's birth. |
|  | So we pray. |
|  | In the agony of unanswered questions and the turmoil of emotions ... |
| All: | God be with us. |
| Leader: | Now we mark \_\_\_\_\_'s journey from his/her pain and distress into the love of God that surpasses our understanding and whose hands will shelter the flame of his/her life for all time. |
| Symbolic action: | the shield is removed from the candle and a family member or friend shelters the flame with her/his hands during final prayer.) |
| Leader: | In our emptiness and helplessness ... |
| All: | God be with us |
| Leader: | To the wonder of God's love, we commit our brother/sister, \_\_\_\_\_. May that love and ours be the sheltering hands that make present to us the flame of life continuing in him/her. We remember, too, the warmth of the love, which reaches out to us today from our family and friends. May we all one day be welcomed into God's fullness of life |

where all sorrow and pain will be extinguished for ever.

Amen.

| | |
|---|---|
| Symbolic | The lit candle is taken away out of the room |
| action: | and no longer seen. |

## (C) *Prayer for family and friends*

Leader:   Where was God when this happened? Why didn't God prevent it? How can I believe in a God of love any more?

All:   We feel angry and in despair.

O God hear our cry!

Leader:   Sometimes our world collapses around us and we feel we can't go on.

Could we have prevented it?

Did s/he think we didn't care?

Should we have realised s/he was so desperate?

Were there signs we missed?

All:   We cry out our questions and our pain as feelings of anger, guilt, fear and shame churn up within us.

O God, hear our cry!

Leader:   It is impossible to get over the loss of a member of the family or a friend, we can only learn to live with the waves of sadness that come and go as our lives continue.

Help us to help each other, by talking and listening, by reaching out for support and giving it, by finding ways of letting our grief enable us to do good for others.

May we rediscover our hopes and dreams as we care for one another.

All:          Keep us day by day and draw us closer to one another and to you, the God of compassion and love.

## (D) *Prayers for the personal use of the bereaved*

*Accepting the sympathy of others:*
Help me to respond warmly, Lord, to the sympathy of my friends and neighbours. Remind me that we most of us feel shy and awkward and don't know what to say. Help me not to imagine that people are being critical and unsympathetic. Help me to explain that I want to talk about _____, even if I get upset, because my memories are important. And if people want to help, give me the gift of accepting graciously. Amen.

*Sorting out clothes and possessions:*
A prayer of remembering in action: recall some of the clothes and possessions that gave him/her pleasure during various stages of his/her life. What happened to them? Are they still in the house or is someone else being warmed or entertained by them? Remember how sizes and styles changed and interests developed or were exhausted?

Gradually, become aware that s/he has no need of all these clothes and possessions now because s/he is clothed with light like the sun. 'Consider the lillies of the field, how they grow they neither toil or spin ...' Maybe you would like to read Matthew 6: 25-34 in the room you are clearing.

Finally, give away with a generous heart being aware of your loved one being glad that others will be helped by your action.

*Choosing mementoes:*
What shall I keep?
Lord, help me to choose thing that will be a window to my memories of _____. May my memories be a way of knowing that s/he will always be a part of my life/ my family and we will always belong to one another and to you.

We may want something tangible to keep and hold or use, but you may find it helpful to recall the music s/he liked and listen to it; the books s/he kept (maybe from childhood), and read them; the activities s/he enjoyed, and take an interest in them.

## 9.4    Formal Prayers

*(Based on Church of Scotland Book of Common Order 1940)*
Opening sentences: Corinthians 1:3-7
Prayers:                    Loving Father, you are the home and dwelling place of all your people from all time and for all generations; come close to us as we come to you under the shadow of our grief and distress for in you alone is our confidence and hope.

God of all comfort, you are the Creator of all and you love everything your hands have made, so draw near to us in our loss and help us to find strength and refuge in you. Keep hold of those who have been bereaved and assure them that you are with them in their anger, despair and doubt; may they

FROM DESPAIR TO HOPE

pass through the stormy waters of grief and find in you their peace: may they walk through the shadow of death and find in you the light of life.

God the Listener, you are the God of forgiveness and acceptance, bring us all into unity with you and with one another in your presence for you are the one from whom we come and to whom we return.

We make these and all our prayers spoken and unspoken in the name of Jesus Christ who gave his life for us. Amen.

*A prayer seeking God*

*The God I Don't Believe In*
I don't believe in a God who wills that a young person should be so distressed that s/he sees death as the only way of escape.

I don't believe in a God who gives such unbearable stress and heavy burdens to someone with a young family to care for that s/he feels that it can no longer be carried.

I don't believe in a God who causes pain and suffering so acute that a sick person cries out for an end to it all.

I don't believe in a God who deprives an old person of all that s/he holds dear so s/he feels that there is nothing to live for.

I believe in God who sets humanity free in a world of many opportunities, who has given us freedom to do good or evil, to use our intelligence to develop ideas and create new things, to enhance the world or to destroy it, to give life and happiness or to take life and cause hate and sadness.

So where is God now? – In the midst of us all
As we struggle to support the young

To build secure relationships,
To relieve the pain and loneliness of the sick and the old,
To comfort the bereaved.
God is with us in our suffering and in our joy,
God's small voice calls to us in the dark and we see the pinpoint of Light.
That is the reality.

## 9.5     Comments on Ritual

Ritual plays an important part in human life. At times the word is used to describe activities that take place in a purely religious context. This, however, is much too narrow a use of the term. For instance, children constantly create rituals as they play; it seems to be one of the important ways in which they learn. Communities from time immemorial have found or created modes of marking significant events through a variety of rituals both religious and non-religious. This is particularly noticeable around such events as birth, the advent of puberty, marriage and death. Ways of observing such events tend to develop a particular pattern or range of patterns in any given society or group. Members of that society then come to expect and recognise these partially structured behaviours. Over time these practices change and evolve. Their function is to observe and mark an event or events that have taken place, relate the events to values that are important to the group and make a way in which the community, group or family can create a sense of togetherness by performing certain familiar actions together – almost like the steps of a dance.

Anthropologists and social scientists suggest that such ritualised behaviour is very important in helping individuals as well as groups to connect with a sense of security and solidarity, to re-emphasise particular values and hence to cope with the events of living and more particularly with significant changes in life.

Psychotherapists and counsellors suggest that individuals or families at times develop particular familiar patterns of behaviour, which while very individualistic can be helpful in coping with change or trauma. They also note that we as humans ritualise in an informal way all the time, and this gives a sense of familiarity, meaning, structure and predictability to our lives. The ritual that is created for instance around Sunday dinner, or a birthday, is a particular illustration of this, differing from household to household but encapsulating certain values and priorities that are important to a particular family. We celebrate and create rituals around graduations, twenty-first birthdays, significant wedding anniversaries as well as many less significant events.

Rituals performed in a community context give a sense of togetherness and unity, and provide a sense of social support and cohesion that is particularly helpful at times of significance, transition or tragedy. The opening of Parliament is an interesting and clear statement of the importance attached to that institution and the values that it encapsulates. At a different level, the events that evolve to mark winning (or losing) the World Cup or other significant sporting occasions also illustrate national or community ritualised behaviours.

We are all familiar with the customary rites of passage that mark important events such as birth, the onset of adolescence, marriage and death. Such rituals still create a sense of togetherness and support as well as usually pointing to wider spiritual or ideological realities. An interesting illustration of this is that even in our increasingly secular and individually orientated society the rituals of the Church are still popular even with those who have only the merest nodding acquaintance with Christian belief and practice. Baptism, confirmation, marriage and funeral rites are still actively observed by huge numbers. In some of the Scandinavian countries where formal Christian practice is particularly low, the state has introduced a very popular community event to mark the passage from childhood to adolescence. This replaces the rite of Confirmation for those who are not believers.

Formal and informal ritual has always had an important place in bereavement. The traditional practices associated with the wake or the Jewish Shiva drew people together to create a sense of support, caring and solidarity at a time of trauma and loss; the particular religious practices provided a framework of meaning and reassurance at such times. Ritual in such contexts creates a framework or 'space' in which to acknowledge and express the sense of emotional trauma and pain. It also points to wider realities that echo the beliefs and aspirations of those who are mourning. Many traditional ritual practices have lost their meaning or value in contemporary society. This opens up possibilities for the creation of new, contemporary practices, or investing the old ones with new life, in ways that are experienced as helpful and appropriate for those involved.

Many therapists and grief counsellors suggest that good or well-designed rituals help the grief-work process significantly. They do not remove the pain; they can, however, offer subtle but very real support.

It is important to recognise the significance of both societal or community rituals as well as individual or small group ritual around death. The two are not mutually exclusive and both should have the flexibility to be useful to those who are most significantly affected.

Bad or poorly designed ritual, or ones that are not experienced as fitting or appropriate for the deceased or the survivors, can be damaging, leaving behind a sense of bitterness and deepened pain. It is particularly important therefore that those who are charged with or have the responsibility for the conduct, facilitation or creation of rituals around death or suicide are sensitive to the wishes,

FROM DESPAIR TO HOPE

needs and values of those who are mourning. Horror stories abound here!

At a personal level I and some other family members still remember with deep pain the sense of exclusion from my mother's funeral, held according to the rites of a denomination to which we did not belong. Little in the service meant anything to me, there had been no consultation and insult was added to injury when I was refused permission to read my mother's favourite scripture portion, as I did not belong to that church.

In another situation, a group of friends and family members wanted to arrange a memorial service for some young people who had died in particularly difficult circumstances. The invited officiant insisted, despite the wishes of the participants, that joy must be the central theme of the service. 'It was a travesty; I needed to mourn with the others, not be forced to sing "happy clappy" songs. I'll never forget it, it was so terrible,' said one parent afterwards. An opportunity for a real acknowledgement of what the group was feeling, and the support that they could have gained from a sensitively and carefully designed and facilitated ritual, had been lost. For rituals to be effective they need to be geared to the group of people who they are seeking to support and facilitate.

In looking at the creation of ritual it is useful to consider firstly the community or religious rituals and secondly the individual or sub-group rituals. Both areas are important and when sensitively handled offer great potential for healing.

In considering either it is important to emphasise two words – *adaptability* and *sensitivity*.

*Adaptability*
The standard liturgies, orders of service or fashions of the moment need not be treated as though they were carved in stone. Instead they can be adapted creatively to the situation at hand and to the needs and values of those who

they are performed to serve. While those who are mourning will probably be both shocked and traumatised, particularly after a death by suicide, with support they may have very clear ideas of how the service may be adapted to reflect both the life of the deceased and their own wants and needs. Offering suggestions, alternatives, possibilities and choices may help them to realise that a meaningful service can be created using the framework of the usual order, or if desirable by putting this aside and creating something completely new.

It is important to recognise that the person who has died may have been a part of a number of groupings. It may not be possible to cater helpfully for all these at one gathering. For instance the school friends or work colleagues of a young person who has died might be usefully helped to design a memorial service that reflects their relationship with the deceased as well as their particular ethos, either sometime after the main funeral service or indeed as part of it. Many bereaved parents as well as the friends involved have found such a service profoundly meaningful as it illustrates both the esteem in which their loved one was held as well as reflecting parts of their personality and experience with which the family may have been less familiar. Often such events have a reality and depth of emotion lacking in more formal rituals. The expression of emotion is a central part of remembering, and in a safe context can aid healing.

*Sensitivity*
Listening to the language both spoken and unspoken, noticing who is being involved in planning and who is being left out, and getting a sense of the range of need of those most closely involved are all important. An explicit or implicit desire to exclude a girl or boy friend, or group of friends, because the family did not approve of them, will need sensitive pastoral handling in both directions, but should not be ignored. Allowing the expression of concern

or hurt will often help and ultimately compromise is often possible.

Likewise creating a service that is full of faith or hope may fit the church's need, but may not reflect the life that was lived or the reality of the bereaved. Using a wonderful set liturgy full of symbols and candles may be deeply unhelpful to those more accustomed to simplicity, extempore prayer and gospel hymns.

In order to be meaningful and useful a service needs to reflect the realities and the emotional experience of those who are present. To gauge all this needs the ability to observe carefully, to listen imaginatively and to facilitate creatively. In the last analysis however a demonstration of deep pastoral caring and sensitivity tends to compensate for other shortcomings.

Using ritual on the journey of grief and healing for individuals, family or other smaller groups can be tremendously positive. This is particularly the case when death has been tragic or where the original funeral was not experienced as helpful. Finding ways of remembering and of sharing memories can be of very real help at various stages such as anniversaries, birthdays or on other significant occasions. Sometimes it is enough to suggest and discuss such possibilities – remember that people once they are introduced to an idea can be very inventive. In other situations a more proactive approach, suggesting a visit to the grave or place of significance, or the use of readings or symbols or meditation or some combination of all this may be appropriate. On occasion what is needed is the sense of a companion who will support and advise in the creation and facilitation of such events.

*An example*
Bernie's twenty-year-old daughter, Geri, died by suicide following the break up of a long-term relationship. She had been quite depressed for some time. While deeply shocked and grief stricken, the family gave themselves

time to think and plan a variety of rituals that would allow them the support they needed as well as echoing something of the richness of Geri's life. They decided to bring her body home before the funeral. Geri had loved and been very involved in the world of dance. Some friends from this part of her life were invited to create a dance of welcome when her body was brought home and another of farewell when she was taken to the church. During the evening other friends and family were invited to call and to share something of what Geri had meant to them. Others who had offered help were asked to bring food. Thought was also given to the funeral service. The church was decorated with wild flowers, Geri's favourite. A number of large pictures of Geri and various items symbolising different parts of her life were placed around the church. Special music was chosen to be played over the church PA system. Bernie herself read a poem at the service and a close friend spoke of Geri's life and death. Joy and pain, remembering, loss and anger were all acknowledged and woven together. The scripture reading, prayer and meditation were all chosen in conjunction with family and friends and to echo the variety of emotions being experienced. People described it as the most meaningful funeral they had ever attended. It did not remove the pain, it did however offer a supportive context for its expression.

## Another example

Jean had battled with depression for some years. On a number of occasions during this time she had felt quite actively suicidal. It wasn't until she sought counselling that she began to relate her depression to the mid-term miscarriage that she had experienced ten years previously. She had lost the baby while going to the toilet, and had flushed the loo before realising what had happened. This trauma was followed by the break up of her long-standing relationship with the baby's father. She had told few people of her pregnancy or miscarriage, had had virtually no support, and had sought to cope by dismissing the whole experience. In therapy she began to recognise and live the huge trauma that she had experienced and that had been largely unacknowledged by herself or anyone else. Following some weeks of deep grieving she recognised that that there was still some unfinished business to attend to. Firstly she felt that she needed to give the baby a name, secondly to acknowledge her presence (Jean instinctively felt the baby had been a girl). Thirdly she felt that it would be important to say goodbye. With the encouragement of her therapist she designed and arranged two rituals. The first involved meeting with a number of close friends and family members to tell them of her experience and to invite them to a naming ceremony. This was held in a quiet place using recorded music, poetry and Scripture readings, and a prayer, in which everyone present participated. Jean then named the baby and after a pause for reflection the group went and ate together. A week later a smaller group met at the seashore, Jean carrying a bunch of five roses, one for each month that she sensed the baby had been alive within her. After reading a verse of poetry the roses were cast on the water as Jean with deep tears bad farewell, supported by her friends, all of whom were deeply moved.

Attending to her own needs through these simple rituals allowed Jean to acknowledge what she needed to, in a supportive and very safe context. This in turn helped her to move on in her own life, while integrating her brief experience of motherhood. She is now at peace around that part of her life.

# APPENDIX A
# – SELECTED RESOURCES

There are many available sources of resources, and further reading, elsewhere. There is no wish to even attempt to replicate that here. Rather the following list is a collection of further material suggested by various contributors to this publication, and, as such, represents the personal choices of the those people. Firstly, however, we list the main contact details for some of the main organisations providing support.

## Organisations

**The Samaritans**
Tel: 1850-60-90-90 (RoI) / 08457-90-90-90 (NI)
Room 35, 112 Marlborough Street, Dublin 1
Tel: 01-872-7700
5 Wellesley Avenue, Belfast BT9 6DG
Tel: 028-906-64422
And regional branches in many other locations through Ireland

## AWARE
72 Lower Leeson Street, Dublin 2
Tel: 01-830-8449 Helpline 01-676-6616
And 30 centres throughout Ireland Many publications available on all aspects of depression, including 'Suicide in Ireland – a global perspective and a national strategy'

## National Suicide Bereavement Support Network
PO Box 1 Youghal, Co Cork
Tel: 024-95561

## Treetops – a children's bereavement group
8 Upper Crescent, Belfast BT7 1NT
Tel: 01232 325008

## Bereavement Counselling Service
Dublin St., Baldoyle, Dublin 13
Tel: 01-8391766
St Ann's Church, Dawson St., Dublin 2
Tel: 01-6767727
And in other centres, mainly in and around Dublin There are also other such services, as well as suicide bereavement support groups, in Dublin, Cork and most of the main cities and towns in Ireland.

## Foyle Search and Rescue
18 Victoria Road, Waterside, 'Derry
Tel: 028-71313800
Activities include a volunteer suicide prevention service

## Age Action Ireland
30-31 Lower Camden Street, Dublin 2
Tel: 01-475-6989

## CRUSE Bereavement Care, Belfast
Helpline: 0870-1671677
Tel: 028-90792419

**Irish Hospice Foundation**
9 Fitzwilliam Place, Dublin 2
Tel: 01-6765599

**The National Suicide Research Foundation**
National University of Ireland, University College, Cork

**Irish Association of Suicidology**
c/o St Mary's Hospital, Castlebar, Co Mayo
Tel: 094-21333

## Worship Material

Wild Goose Worship Group
*Stages on the Way*
Wild Goose Publications, Glasgow 1998

*The Last Journey*
*Wee Worship Book* (Revised)
Wild Goose Publications, Glasgow 2000

*Landscapes of Light – An illustrated anthology of prayers*
David Adams, with photography by Robert Cooper
SPCK, 2001
ISBN 0281053200

## Novels

*Veronika Decides to Die*
Paolo Coelho
Harper Collins, 2000
ISBN 0722540442

*Roxanna Slade*
Reynolds Price
Scribness Book Company, 1998
ISBN 0684832925

## Other Publications

*Good Grief*
Sydney Callaghan
Collins, 1990
ISBN 0 00-627488 9
2nd edn, Colourpoint Books, 1999
ISBN 1-898392 51 X

*Young People and Suicide*
Louise Hurley and Fran Bissett
Irish Youthwork Press, 1995
ISBN 0 9522207 7 6

*An analysis particularly in relation to youth suicide, with many facts and figures, and a chapter devoted to an extensive list of relevant services and resources.*

*Suicide Bereavement and Loss – Perspectives and Responses*
Edited by Luke Monahan
The Irish Association of Pastoral Care in Education, 1999
ISBN 0 9530315 35

*Media Guidelines on Portrayal of Suicide*
The Samaritans and The Irish Association of Suicidology, 2000

*Echoes of Suicide*
Edited by Siobhán Foster Ryan and Luke Monahan
Veritas, 2001
ISBN 1 853 9050 46

*The Bereavement Journey*
Gregory Allen
Messenger Publications, 2000

*Responding to Youth Suicide* and *Attempted Youth Suicide in Ireland*
Barnardos, Christchurch Square, Dublin 8 Tel: 01-4530355
ISBN 1898662525

*A Special Scar – experiences of people bereaved by suicide*
Alison Wertheimer
Routledge Press, 2001
ISBN 0 415 220270

*Suicide Prevention in Schools – Best Practice Guidelines*
Irish Association of Suicidology (see address above)

*Report of National Task Force on Suicide*
Department of Health and Children, Dublin 1998
ISBN 0 7076 4965 X

### Video
*The Suicide of Young People and its Impact on the Family*
This training pack is available from Concord Video and Film Council Ltd, Rosehill Centre, 22 Hines Road, Ipswich, Suffolk IP3 9BG priced at £300.00 plus VAT.

This 20-videotape training pack has been developed by Prof. Malcolm Brown and Dr Heather Ferguson-Brown and comprises video interviews with 19 family members whose close young relatives have taken their own lives, together with a 45 minute interview with Dr Colin Murray-Parkes on the subject of suicide of young people and its impact on, and the needs of, family members experiencing such a bereavement. It is a resource for trainers offering courses for a range of professions and voluntary organisations working in the field of suicide of young people, prevention and bereavement.

# APPENDIX B
# – A PERSONAL
# RESOURCE LIST

Readers may find it useful to draw up their own personal resource list. This will reflect useful local contact points and sources of information and advice, ready to hand for an emergency situation.

| Who | Name | Phone number or contact details |
|---|---|---|
| **Trusted Friends** | | |
| | | |
| **Doctors** | | |
| **Hospitals** | | |
| **Health Centre** | | |
| **Children's Helpline** | | |
| **Ambulance** | | |

| Who | Name | Phone number or contact details |
|---|---|---|
| Police Station | | |
| School | | |
| Other Counsellors | | |
| | | |
| Specialist | | |
| Health Services | | |
| | | |
| Local Clergy | | |

# APPENDIX C – BIOGRAPHICAL NOTES ON CONTRIBUTORS

**May Anderson** – retired social worker; member of the Board of Social Witness of the Presbyterian Church in Ireland.

**Berta Armitage** – farms with her husband in County Tipperary; member of the Council on Social Responsibility of the Methodist Church in Ireland.

**Malcolm Brown and Heather Ferguson-Brown** – Malcolm Brown was Professor of Social Work at Queen's University, Belfast, for many years and is currently Visiting Professor at Lincoln University. Heather Ferguson-Brown is a Senior Lecturer in Social Work, also at Lincoln University.

**Sydney Callaghan** – Methodist Minister (deceased 2001); former president of Methodist Church; lifelong supporter of Samaritans (founded the Belfast branch) and concerned with pastoral care of those touched by suicide.

**Robert Cochran** – Hon. Secretary, Council on Social Responsibility, Methodist Church in Ireland. Chair, Department of Social Issues, Irish Inter-Church Meeting. Professionally he is a Chartered Statistician and Chartered (Software) Engineer.

**Edith Loane** – psychiatrist; past World President, World Federation of Methodist and Uniting Church Women; Member of the Council on Social Responsibility of the Methodist Church in Ireland.

**Katherine Meyer** – Member of the ecumenical chaplaincy team in Trinity College Dublin, representing the Presbyterian and Methodist Churches in Ireland. She is an ordained minister in the Presbyterian Church in Ireland, and has worked in both Belfast and Dublin in congregational and community ministries. Originally from the USA, she is a graduate of Yale Divinity School.

**David Neilands** – Methodist Minister; for many years the General Secretary of the Department of Youth and Children's Work of the Methodist Church in Ireland; currently the Chaplain to Methodist College Belfast.

**Joan Rippingale** – Marriage and Relationship Counsellor; member of Parents Support Group of Gay and Lesbian Switchboard; Facilitator in Communication on Relationship and Sexuality; Member of the Council on Social Responsibility of the Methodist Church in Ireland

**Salters Sterling** – Formerly Academic Secretary, Trinity College Dublin. Member of the Council of the Irish School of Ecumenics and of its steering committee, and of the executive board of the ISE at TCD. Chairman of the Central Council of the Federated Dublin Voluntary Hospitals, member of the Board of the National Children's Hospital, member of the Joint Research Committee of the Federated Hospitals and St James Hospital, part-time lecturer in Ethics for Oncology Nurses in St Luke's Hospital Educational Centre.

**Pam Stotter** – Lecturer in Ecumenical Studies, Irish School of Ecumenics; specialist interests include liturgy and composition of resource material for worship.

**Tony Walsh** – Psychotherapist with a particular interest in grief and loss; Co-founder of the Institute of Psychosocial Medicine in Dublin; lecturer at the Centre for Adult and Community Education at the National University of Ireland, Maynooth; Member of the Council on Social Responsibility of the Methodist Church in Ireland.